"Anxiety is a disorder which can usually be treated effectively,"
say the authors of this book.

Now let *Anxiety and Its Treatment* show you how.

- Take the "Fear Questionnaire" to help see if your anxieties are normal or if you need treatment
- Let the "Obsessive-Compulsive" checklist help you determine if you are *too* concerned with cleaning or other behavior patterns
- Read the chapter on medications for general guidelines on antianxiety prescription drugs, information on how diet may affect different medications, interactions between drugs, and more
- Learn—in detail—how the various types of available psychotherapy may help you with your anxieties
- And get the answers to your questions on children's fears, panic attacks, frightening obsessions, phobias, and more.

For people who feel anxious, those wondering whether they need treatment, patients already receiving professional help, and the families and friends of those suffering from anxiety...

ANXIETY AND ITS TREATMENT

Also by John H. Greist, M.D. and
James W. Jefferson, M.D.

Depression and Its Treatment

Published by
WARNER BOOKS

ANXIETY
AND ITS
TREATMENT

HELP IS AVAILABLE

Advice from three leading psychiatrists
in the field of anxiety treatment

**JOHN H. GREIST, M.D.,
JAMES W. JEFFERSON, M.D.,
& ISAAC M. MARKS, M.D.**

WARNER BOOKS

A Warner Communications Company

Note: The authors have worked to ensure that all information in this book concerning drug dosages, schedules, and routes of administration is accurate at the time of publication and consistent with standards set by the United States Food and Drug Administration and the general medical community. As medical research and practice advance, however, therapeutic standards may change. For this reason, and because human and mechanical errors sometimes occur, we recommend that readers follow the advice of a physician directly involved in their care or the care of a member of their family.

WARNER BOOKS EDITION

This Warner Books Edition is published by arrangement with American Psychiatric Press, Inc., 1400 K Street, N.W., Washington, DC 20005

Books published by the American Psychiatric Press, Inc., represent the views and opinions of the individual authors and do not necessarily reflect the policies and opinions of the Press or the American Psychiatric Association.

Cover design by Anthony Russo

Warner Books, Inc.
666 Fifth Avenue
New York, N.Y. 10103

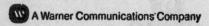 A Warner Communications Company

Printed in the United States of America

First Warner Books Printing: February, 1987

10 9 8 7 6 5 4

To
Revere, Alexandra, Lara, Shaun,
James, Lara, Rafi

who inspire us in many ways

Contents

Contents

About the Authors

DRS. Greist and Jefferson are trained as internists as well as psychiatrists. They are now Professors of Psychiatry at the University of Wisconsin Medical School in Madison, Wisconsin. Dr. Marks is Professor of Experimental Psychopathology at the Institute of Psychiatry in London, England.

Dr. Greist is co-Director of the Anxiety Disorders Center and co-Director of the Lithium Information Center with Dr. Jefferson. He is coauthor with Thomas Greist of *Antidepressant Treatment: The Essentials* (Williams and Wilkins, 1979).

Dr. Jefferson is Director of the Center for Affective Disorders. He and Dr. Greist have coauthored two professional books on lithium: *Primer of Lithium Therapy* (Williams and Wilkins, 1977) and *Lithium Encyclopedia for Clinical Practice,* Second Edition with Deborah Ackerman and Judith Carroll (American Psychiatric Press, Inc., 1986). They also edited *Treatment of Mental Disorders* with Robert L. Spitzer

(Oxford University Press, 1982). Their lay book *Depression and Its Treatment: Help for the Nation's #1 Mental Problem* (American Psychiatric Press, Inc., 1984) is in its second printing.

Dr. Greist and Dr. Jefferson both are regular runners and have five children (two of whom are sick at any given time), two wives (both healthy), three living parents, two dogs, three cars, countless bicycles, and the usual array of problems that affect humankind.

Dr. Marks has conducted research on Anxiety Disorders for the past 20 years and is Director of the Nurse-Therapist Training Program, which has spread to three other sites in England. Among his books are: *Fears and Phobias* (Heinemann Medical-Academic Press, 1969), *Clinical Anxiety* (with Malcolm Lader; Heinemann Medical-Academic Press, 1971), *Living With Fear* (McGraw-Hill, 1978), *Cure and Care of Neuroses* (Wiley, 1981) and *Fears, Phobias and Rituals* (Oxford University Press, 1986). Dr. Marks is married, has two children, and is an avid gardener and hiker.

Acknowledgments

THIS book includes contributions from many clinicians and patients. We can acknowledge the clinicians by name and take pleasure in doing so:

From the Department of Psychiatry at the University of Wisconsin: Richard Anderson, Nancy Barklage, Barbara Calhoun, David Crawford, John Marshall, David Mays, William McKinney, Eben McClenahan, Janet Medenwald, Michael Moran, Teri Perse, and Reid Taylor.

From elsewhere: Stewart Agras, Stanford University; John W. Greist, Thomas Greist, and Anne Greist, Indianapolis, Indiana; Malcolm Lader, Institute of Psychiatry, London; Donald Klein, Columbia University; and David Sheehan, University of South Florida.

Our patients carefully read and criticized drafts of this book. They suggested many of the subjects addressed and the questions asked and answered. We appreciate their important perspective as much as we admire their courage and resilience in facing and overcoming anxiety.

Georgia Greist and Bill Marten sharpened their editors' pencils to clarify our cryptic exposition and expunge our medical metaphors and jargon. It is obvious they did not work on the previous sentence.

Jean Clatworthy prepared the numerous drafts of this book. Her attention to detail, efficiency, and good humor in the face of deadlines constantly enhanced our effectiveness.

Parts of Chapter 3 are condensations of the relevant sections of *Fears, Phobias and Rituals* by Isaac Marks (Oxford University Press, 1986).

The American Psychiatric Press has in five short years become a major publishing house for psychiatric titles. We admire the professionalism of the staff and appreciate the simultaneous care and speed with which they work. Jessica Morgan, who recently left the Press, has our thanks for finding and putting us in touch with people who have been helpful; Ron McMillen has our sympathy for being in the line of fire from people who oppose our positions and interpretations of the scientific literature. Special thanks are due Tim Clancy, whose compulsivity at proofreading matches ours. We take pleasure in sharing responsibility with him for errors in spelling and syntax while retaining responsibility for decisions about content and emphasis.

Introduction

This book is for:
• People who feel anxious
• People being treated for anxiety
• People considering treatment for anxiety
• People wondering whether their anxiety needs treatment
• Families and friends
• Those who treat anxious patients
• And anyone else interested in anxiety

It is a guide to understanding:
• Anxiety
• What anxiety is not
• How anxiety is treated
• Treatment side effects and how they are managed

We wrote it because we know:

- Doctors* sometimes forget to ask patients about important information
- Doctors sometimes forget to advise patients about important facts
- Patients sometimes forget important information
- Patients sometimes misunderstand important instructions
- Fewer than 25 percent of people with anxiety disorders are being treated

We hope it will:

- Maximize the recognition and proper treatment of anxiety
- Minimize treatment difficulties
- Promote the best results for patients

John H. Greist
James W. Jefferson
Madison, Wisconsin

Isaac Marks
London, England

---

* We often use the word *doctor* to indicate psychiatrists and other medical doctors (M.D.'s and D.O.'s), as well as psychologists who have doctor of philosophy degrees (Ph.D.'s). M.D.'s can prescribe medications as well as provide all other treatments for anxiety, including psychotherapy and behavior therapy (or behavioral psychotherapy as it is called in the United Kingdom), while psychologists use psychotherapy and behavior therapy but not drug treatment.

1

What Is Anxiety?

EACH of us has experienced anxiety and fear. To live without them is impossible. Anxiety can be a wearing stress or a stimulating tonic. Fear can be protective and lead to appropriate escape from danger. Fear can be overcome with bravery or be overwhelming. The English language is full of words to describe the many shades of anxiety and fear: aghast, agitation, alarm, anguish, apprehension, concern, consternation, disquiet, distress, dread, fright, horror, misgiving, nervousness, panic, qualm, scare, terror, threatened, trepidation, troubled, unease, unnerved, unsettled, upset, wary.

THE OVERLAP BETWEEN ANXIETY AND FEAR

These terms (*anxiety* and *fear*) have been defined in various ways, some of which are specific and scientific and others of which are vague and overlapping.

We feel that it would be futile to try to impose a rigid definition on either term and that to do so would be more confusing than enlightening. Anxiety and fear are often used interchangeably without any loss of understanding. For example, a phobia is a type of anxiety yet is defined as a "persistent or irrational fear." Or a person may complain of being anxious in anticipation of a specific external event such as public speaking or may have an "ill-defined fear" that something unpleasant will happen.

If any distinction is to be made, it is that the causes of fear tend to be more external to the individual and thus more easily identified, such as when our car skids out of control on a patch of ice or we are threatened by a hoodlum. Anxiety, by contrast, can be viewed as a response to a less obvious, ill-defined, irrational, distant, or unrecognized source of danger. *Anxiety* describes an unpleasant state of mental (or psychological) tension often accompanied by physical (or physiological) symptoms in which we may feel both physically and mentally helpless, exhausted by being always on guard against an unidentifiable danger. *Fear* also causes unpleasant mental tension and physical changes.

Phobias are recognized by the sufferer as irrational fears that do not frighten most people and that cause the sufferer to avoid the frightening situation or even thoughts about it.

Anxious people have some of the following common complaints: shakiness, jumpiness, jitteriness, trembling, tension, muscle aches, fatigue, and inability to relax. There may also be eyelid twitch, furrowed brow, strained face, fidgeting, restlessness, easy startle, and sighing.

Other indications of anxiety are sweating, racing or pounding heart, cold, clammy hands, dry mouth, dizziness, light-headedness, numbness and/or tingling in the hands or feet or other parts of the body, upset stomach, hot or cold spells, frequent need to urinate, diarrhea, discomfort in the pit of the stomach, lump in the throat, flushing, pallor, and a high pulse and respiration rate, even while resting.

An anxious person is apprehensive and continually feels anxious, worries, ruminates, and anticipates that something bad will happen to himself or herself (such as fainting, losing control, or dying) or to others (such as family members becoming ill or being injured in an accident).

The individual feels "on edge," impatient, or irritable. There may be complaints of being easily distracted or having difficulty concentrating and sleeping.

DIFFERENT KINDS OF ANXIETY AND PANIC

Anxiety has many gradations of intensity. It can be a mere qualm, rise to marked trembling, or become complete panic. Panic is extremely intense anxiety.

The onset and duration of anxiety (or panic) also varies. It may come on gradually over minutes or hours, or strike like lightning out of the blue. And it may last for only a few seconds or for hours or even days, although severe panic does not usually last longer than half an hour or so.

If we feel anxious or panicky regardless of where we are, that is called *spontaneous anxiety* (or *spontaneous panic* if it is very intense). Anxiety which occurs only in particular situations is called *situational* or *phobic anxiety* (or *phobic panic* if it is severe). And if our anxiety is triggered even by merely thinking of particular situations, that is a variety of phobic anxiety (or phobic panic) which is called *anticipatory anxiety* (or *anticipatory panic*).

As far as we can tell, the feelings are similar whether the anxiety (or panic) is spontaneous or phobic. Research has found that the type of phobia also makes little difference to the feelings that are experienced: People with agoraphobia, social phobia, and animal phobia (which will be explained in Chapter 2) all report similar feelings when in the phobic situation.

Intensity, however, can pull out more stops, depending on the type of anxiety or panic. In experiencing mild tension we might have no more than an unpleasant feeling in the pit

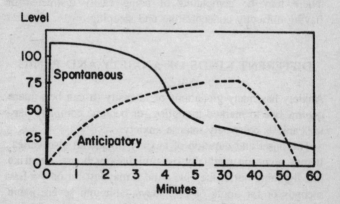

Figure 1. A graphic representation of the rise and fall of spontaneous anxiety (or panic) versus anticipatory anxiety (or panic). Spontaneous anxiety comes on unpredictably, "out of the blue," peaks almost immediately, and then gradually fades. Anticipatory anxiety builds gradually up to the time of encounter with something that is feared and then drops sharply.

of our stomach. The extreme anxiety we call panic brings out a greater orchestration of feelings—we are more likely then to feel rapid heartbeat, sweating, and trembling and to think that we are going mad or losing control.

Panic and anticipatory anxiety can usually be differentiated, and most individuals grow in their ability to do so as their experience with anxiety/panic increases. Figure 1 symbolically displays the subjective difference patients often describe between the two anxieties (this illustration was prepared by Dr. David Sheehan, who has kindly allowed us to reproduce it here). Other patients report little, if any, difference in the subjective experience or signs of panic and anticipatory anxiety.

All in all, it is simply not necessary to make a big fuss about distinguishing between anxiety and fear. Understanding and benefiting from this book does not require rigid definitions, so we suggest that you proceed without further fear or anxiety.

ANXIETY IN HISTORY

Hippocrates (460–377 B.C.) described a height phobic man who could not cross over bridges or even stand beside a shallow ditch. Robert Burton described phobias in *Anatomy of Melancholy* (1621):

> [There was a patient who would] not walk alone from home, for fear he should swoon, or die. A second [man] fears every man he meets will rob him, quarrel with him, or kill him. A third dare not venture to walk alone, for fear he should meet the devil, a thief, be sick . . . another dares not go over a bridge, come near a pool, brook, steep hill, lye in

a chamber where cross-beams are, for fear he be tempted to hang, drown or precipitate himself. If he be in a silent auditory, as at a sermon, he is afraid he shall speak aloud, at unawares, something indecent, unfit to be said. If he be locked in a close room, he is afraid of being stifled for want of air, and still carried bisket, aquavitae, or some strong waters about him, for fear of deliquiums [fainting], or being sick; or if he be in a throng, middle of a church, multitude, where he may not well get out, though he sit at ease, he is so misaffected.

Burton also identified phobic figures from history such as Augustus Caesar, who was afraid of the dark, and Demosthenes and Tully, who experienced stage fright.

From Burton onward, descriptions of phobias became commonplace. A contemporary of James I of England teased that the King's fear of swords was so great that "Elizabeth was King, James I was Queen" (A. Le Camus, *Medicine de l'Esprit*, vol. 1, pp. 259–265, Paris, 1769).

In 1721 a physician described phobias of syphilis:

If but a pimple appears or any slight ache is felt, they distract themselves with terrible apprehensions: by which means they make life uneasy to themselves and run for help. . . . And so strongly are they for the most part possessed with this notion that an honest practitioner generally finds it more difficult to cure the imaginary evil than the real one. (I. MacAlpine, "Syphilophobia," *British Journal of Venereal Disease*, vol. 33, 1957, pp. 92–99)

During his thirties, Sigmund Freud had many anxiety symptoms, including fears of travel.

CHILDREN'S FEARS

Everyone who has raised children is aware how common are their irrational fears. Fears wax and wane, and the patterns of change—while not identical between children—follow a common path which can be described with recognizable accuracy. The usual causes for children's fears and anxieties are nicely, if oversimply, summarized in Table 1.

The changes in children's fears that develop with age are shown in Figure 2. Infants fear unfamiliar things, while young schoolchildren fear imaginary creatures and fear for their personal safety. Later, social anxieties about personal relationships and performing in front of others begin to become more prominent. When children's fears occur outside the ages suggested in Table 1—or when they are very severe or persistent to the point of causing handicap—then evaluation by a doctor is worthwhile.

ANXIETY AND ANXIETY DISORDERS

It is important to realize that distressing anxiety is not confined to formal psychiatric disorders. Anxiety may be a normal response to many threatening life situations, including medical illness. Just where "normal" anxiety ends and "abnormal" anxiety begins may be difficult to determine. Doctors often use criteria such as severity, duration, association with other symptoms, and appropriateness of the anxiety to make this distinction.

It stands to reason that the more severe, long-standing, and incapacitating anxiety is, the more likely it will require treatment. Once you read more about the Anxiety Disorders in Chapter 2, the need for treatment of these conditions will be evident. On the other hand, we do not mean to imply that

Table 1. Usual Causes of Fears or Anxiety Among Children and Adolescents

Age	Source of Fears or Anxiety
0–6 months	Loss of support, loud noises
7–12 months	Strangers, heights; sudden, unexpected, and looming objects
1 year	Separation from parent; toilet, injury, strangers
2 years	A multitude of sources, including loud noises (vacuum cleaners, sirens/alarms, trucks, and thunder), animals (e.g., large dogs), dark room, separation from parent, large objects or machines, change in personal environment, strange peers
3 years	Masks, dark, animals, separation from parent
4 years	Separation from parent, animals, dark, noises (including at night)
5 years	Animals, "bad" people, dark, separation from parent, bodily harm
6 years	Supernatural beings (e.g., ghosts, witches, "Darth Vader"), bodily injuries, thunder and lightning, dark, sleeping or staying alone, separation from parent
7–8 years	Supernatural beings, dark, media events (e.g., news reports on the threat of nuclear war or child kidnapping), staying alone, bodily injury
9–12 years	Tests and examinations in school, school performance, bodily injury, physical appearance, thunder and lightning, death, dark
Teens	Social performance, sexuality

Modified and reproduced from *Treating Children's Fears and Phobias: A Behavioral Approach*, by R. Morris and T. Kratochwill (copyright © 1983 Pergamon Press; reproduced with permission).

milder anxiety not amounting to a disorder should never be treated. There are many occasions when brief counseling and/or the judicious short-term use of an antianxiety drug can be quite beneficial in reducing suffering and hastening

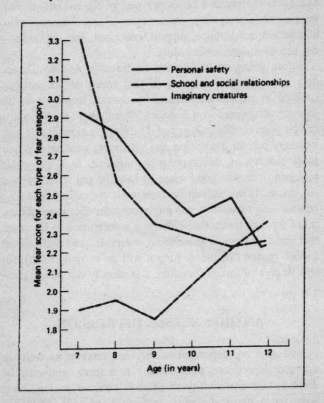

Figure 2. Changes in the causes of children's fears that develop with age. Fears about imaginary creatures and personal safety are quite frequent in seven-year-olds. As these fade, fears about school and social relationships begin to increase. Reproduced with permission of Jean B. Goldsmith, Ph.D.

recovery. For example, a certain degree of anxiety almost always occurs in the first few days following a heart attack. While this response is seldom severe enough to be considered abnormal, many doctors believe that the reduction of excessive anxiety is a necessary part of the overall care of the patient. Therapeutic interventions in such instances usually include reassurance, support, education, and—at times— the use of an antianxiety drug.

Before going on to describe the specific Anxiety Disorders, we want to stress again that much of the anxiety suffered by people and treated by doctors would never be formally diagnosed as a disorder. Nonetheless, such anxiety can be painful, disturbing, and disabling; anxiety of this sort warrants careful evaluation and, at times, treatment. Since most anxiety of this type is in response to a particular problem, it makes good sense to identify and try to correct the cause. If this cannot be done or if correcting the cause takes a long time, then you might consider obtaining anxiety relief through treatment. Finally, it is important to be aware that most anxiety is reasonable, tolerable, and self-limited (which means that before long it will go away by itself); for this degree of anxiety, treatment is usually not necessary.

ANXIETY VERSUS DEPRESSION

People who are depressed usually feel anxious as well. In agitated depression, their anxiety is extreme and may be displayed as an inability to sit still, constant pacing, hand wringing, picking at clothing or fingers and nails, lip biting, and anguished facial expressions that convey their inner turmoil. Depression may accentuate anxiety and worry about everyday problems that individuals previously took in stride.

Difficulty making up one's mind and other indications of anxiety may also emerge with depression.

On the other hand, anxiety itself is depressing, and it is normal to get somewhat depressed if anxiety persists too long. Usually, however, sad feelings in anxious people are less intense than those found in people in whom depression is the primary problem. Relieving primary anxiety often helps mild associated depression as well.

Some people can have both a primary depression and a primary Anxiety Disorder. For doctors, it is current practice to distinguish the various types of depression and anxiety based on information obtained from the patient: the medical history of the individual and his or her family, the specific symptoms that are present, and sometimes the sequence of symptoms (that is, whether depression or anxiety occurs first). The doctor's professional decision on whether anxiety or depression or another disorder is the primary cause of a patient's difficulty is called the *differential diagnosis*. At times, however, arriving at this differential diagnosis is complicated and may require repeated evaluations through interviews, laboratory tests, and—sometimes—trials of various treatments appropriate for depression and Anxiety Disorders.

ANXIETY CAUSED BY MEDICAL ILLNESS, MEDICINES, AND OTHER CAUSES

Although it is uncommon, a number of medical problems can produce anxiety. Because anxiety affects many organ systems (cardiovascular, respiratory, neurological, gastrointestinal, urinary, etc.), patients and doctors may focus on the problems in one organ system and miss seeing the overall pattern. It is possible for medical doctors to sometimes overlook Anxiety Disorders and over-investigate possible medical causes for symptoms that are actually caused by anxiety. In the same way, psychiatrists and psychologists who are attuned to listening to complaints related to anxiety may miss an underlying medical problem that is causing them.

In the cardiovascular system, pain from an insufficient blood supply to the heart muscle can occur either in the form of *angina pectoris* (in which the heart's need for oxygen carried by the blood exceeds the supply available through narrowed coronary arteries that supply blood to the heart muscle itself) or an *acute myocardial infarction*, or heart attack (in which the blood supply is so badly cut off by narrowing or complete blockage of a coronary artery that some heart muscle dies); in either case great anxiety may occur. *Arrhythmias*, in which the heart beats either irregularly or too rapidly or slowly may cause anxiety by producing alarming palpitations and/or reducing the blood supply to the heart muscle itself or to the rest of the body. *Congestive heart failure*, in which the heart is unable to supply the body's needs for blood and the oxygen it carries, may also provoke anxiety. Very low blood pressure or *shock* (in which insufficient effective blood volume is present to supply the body's tissues with oxygen and other essential substances) can raise anxiety. In these instances of cardiovascular disorder, anxiety can alert a person to the primary cardiovascular problem; relief of the primary problem by medical treatment helps relieve the anxiety it has been causing. In such cases treatment should be directed primarily at the cardiovascular problem.

Respiratory problems—including recurrent attacks of *asthma*, chronic lung diseases such as *emphysema*, and acute problems such as *pulmonary embolism* (in which a blood clot blocks part of the blood flow through a lung and decreases the amount of oxygen that can be absorbed into the circulating blood from that part of the lung—can all heighten anxiety. Again, relief of the primary respiratory disorder usually reduces the resulting anxiety, whereas treatments for Anxiety Disorders alone would be ineffective and could leave the potentially serious primary problem untreated.

Neurologic problems, including *encephalopathy* (brain dysfunction from a variety of causes) and *seizure disorder* (epilepsy), may cause anxiety. Sometimes a benign neurological disorder such as *familial tremor* (a nonprogressive inherited disorder) may be mistaken for anxiety disorder. Sensations that the world or the person are spinning (*vertigo*) are very distressing and frequently produce anxiety.

Disorders of the hematologic (blood) and immune systems may produce anxiety, as in *anemia*, when too little oxygen is carried by the blood, or when the immune system overreacts in acute *anaphylactic shock*, or with certain chronic immune diseases which may affect the brain's blood vessels.

Several endocrine or hormonal disorders can give rise to anxiety. Among them *diabetes* (too little insulin), *hypothyroidism* and *hyperthyroidism* (too little or too much thyroid hormone, respectively), *parathyroid disease* (which causes changes in calcium and phosphorus levels), *Cushing's disease* (too much hormone from the outer part of the adrenal gland) and *pheochromocytoma* (too much hormone from the center of the adrenal gland) may all cause pronounced anxiety.

Medications prescribed by physicians or purchased "over the counter" may also cause anxiety symptoms. Stimulants, digitalis, thyroid supplements, cold medicines, diet pills, antispasmodic medications, and—paradoxically—antidepressants given to reduce panic may all cause anxiety. Discontinuation of a variety of drugs, including antianxiety drugs (minor tranquilizers), sleeping pills, and certain blood pressure medicines may cause withdrawal symptoms which include prominent anxiety.

Certain dietary excesses or deficiencies may lead to anxiety. The most common offenders are caffeine and caffeine-like substances which are found in coffees, teas, and many soft drinks (see the October 1981 issue of *Consumer Reports* for details on the caffeine content of various beverages). Individual sensitivity varies widely, and some people become anxious with a few cups of coffee or tea or cans of caffeinated soft drink while others may tolerate large amounts without symptoms. Caffeine-containing soft drinks may be an unrecognized cause of anxiety, restlessness, and sleep difficulty in adolescents and especially in younger children. The jitteriness precipitated by caffeine may amount to panic in some individuals, and those with Panic Disorder seem more sensitive to caffeine as well as to a variety of other alerting substances such as some over-the-counter cold preparations. Extreme vitamin deficiencies (which are exceedingly rare) may also lead to anxiety.

Alcohol in its many forms (beer, wine, hard liquor) is a well-recognized yet consistently underdiagnosed cause of anxiety. Patients may minimize or completely exclude their alcohol use from their medical history, and doctors sometimes neglect to ask. Both the excessive consumption of alcohol and withdrawal from alcohol (hangover, shakes, and D.T.'s) can be associated with anxiety. This can be especially troublesome, since some people misuse alcohol in an ill-advised attempt to treat an anxiety problem.

Each of these "medical" causes of anxiety has different symptoms, signs, and sometimes laboratory tests which can point to the correct diagnosis. Careful history taking, physical examination, and laboratory tests as indicated are the keys to finding and resolving medical causes of anxiety.

Although these medical problems are seldom the cause of severe anxiety, they should be identified, since some are life-threatening and may be treated with benefit if discovered early. The anxiety associated with taking or discontinuing certain drugs and other substances can be easily relieved, but only if the cause is recognized. Providing your doctor with a complete history is essential.

EVOLVING THEORIES OF ANXIETY

In psychoanalytic theory, anxiety is thought to represent a conflict hidden beneath the level of conscious awareness. These anxieties are thought by psychoanalysts to have early origins related to discomfort (as when children are sick, soiled, hungry, or frightened), sex (classically involving feelings of the infant and child for its parents), or aggression (sometimes in the various forms of child abuse). Quite logically, this theory led to psychotherapies whose purpose was to first uncover and then resolve the hidden conflict with the expectation that the symptoms symbolizing the conflict would then disappear.

Later it became clear that understanding and resolving less conscious conflicts did not always relieve phobic and obsessive-compulsive anxiety or restore individuals to normal functioning. Learning theorists proposed that anxiety is a learned behavior and, therefore, could be unlearned. Simply put, if a person feels anxious in a situation, avoids it, and so decreases his anxiety, this makes it more likely that the person will try to switch off the anxiety the next time by avoiding again. This relief is bought at a cost of avoiding the feared situation and all the handicaps such avoidance brings on. However, if anxiety-provoking situations are persistently confronted rather than avoided, people

"learn" that their anxiety dies down even without avoidance. Learning theory does not explain why persistent exposure to the feared situation causes the anxiety to subside.

Recently, scientists have focused attention on biochemical
mechanisms that may underlie Anxiety Disorders. Their
theories suggest that certain types of biochemical imbalances are responsible for these disorders and that treatment
directed at correcting such imbalances will be clinically
beneficial. While treatment based on this model is often
assumed to be accomplished only with drugs, it is important
to recognize that psychological and behavioral influences
can cause changes in brain chemistry, and that the biochemical model favors no single therapeutic approach. To the
adage, "For every twisted thought a twisted molecule," we
might add, "For every straightened thought a straightened
molecule."

Of these theories of anxiety (psychodynamic, learning,
and biochemical), as well as genetic (dealing with inheri-
tance) and developmental (issues regarding maturation) theories, each has something to contribute to our understanding
of Anxiety Disorders. The origins of fears are sometimes
identifiable in a patient's past; fears are probably maintained,
in part, by learned avoidance behavior; and Anxiety Disorders have biochemical underpinnings that govern the kind
and extent of anxiety experienced. Some anxieties are clearly influenced by genetic factors, and some anxieties appear
and disappear at common stages in human development. It
is unlikely that any one theory can explain the origins and
maintenance of anxiety. However, theories often generate
sectarian beliefs that introduce and maintain bias in what
should be broad and objective scientific thinking. Sir
Rabindranath Tagore defined a sectarian as "one who thinks
he has the whole sea ladled into his own private pond."
Theorists who become sectarians resemble dogmatists ev-

erywhere. When theory and reality are in conflict, dogmatists impose theory and mistakenly proclaim a fit.

Theory suggests leads that have to be explored and carefully evaluated in rigorous scientific studies. Modesty is appropriate at this stage in our quest for knowledge about the causes of Anxiety Disorders and the mechanisms through which they become manifest, for there still remains much to learn. While theories guide practice and may be helpful to doctors and their patients in providing a rationale for a treatment approach, rationales are often mere rationalizations, theories are often wrong (at least in part), and treatments based on theories can be ineffective (as in some psychoanalytic treatment of Phobic and Obsessive-Compulsive Disorders) or even harmful (when clinicians who believe too strongly in a single theory advocate an ineffective treatment and fail to refer patients for an alternative treatment that could be more effective).

The origins of Anxiety Disorders are complex and still largely beyond our present knowledge. We know, however, how to help many people who have the disorders. Often, effective treatments in medicine are based on experience, as is true for behavioral and drug treatments of anxiety. The explanation for why they are helpful often come after they have been developed rather than before. Practically speaking, we would rather have a treatment that works and not understand why than know the cause of an illness but not be able to effectively treat it.

2

The Anxiety Disorders

THE *prevalence* of a disorder is a measure (usually a percentage) of how frequently that disorder occurs among a representative sample of the population. The prevalence of Anxiety Disorders has recently been assessed by the National Institute of Mental Health. Researchers in three cities (New Haven, Connecticut; Baltimore, Maryland; and St. Louis, Missouri) carefully interviewed nearly 10,000 people and found that 19 percent of those interviewed had at least one psychiatric disorder during the preceding six months. More people suffered from Anxiety Disorders (8.3 percent) than any other problem, and only 23 percent of the people with Anxiety Disorders were receiving treatment. Other studies of prevalence of Anxiety Disorders have found similar but somewhat lower percentages. Remembering the examples of childhood phobias and fears that almost all of us suffered to some degree, the interesting question is not why so many adults have Anxiety Disorders, but how most of us have managed to overcome such problems.

DIAGNOSING MENTAL DISORDERS

Diagnosis serves several purposes. It helps doctors classify disorders according to their cause and predict their course (*prognosis*), select appropriate treatments for disorders, and communicate with patients and other professionals about them. Diagnosis also permits grouping of patients with the same or similar disorders so that the disorders can be better studied and treated.

Diagnosis is often closely linked to theory. Theory can help the design of a diagnostic system if the theory is close to the reality it attempts to explain. Where theory and reality are far apart, however, the value of linking them is diminished; in these cases, it may be helpful to untie diagnosis from theory altogether.

American psychiatry has recently gone through the process of advancing beyond a limited diagnostic system based on psychodynamic theories to a system based on more observable *symptoms* (the feelings and thoughts patients complain of) and *signs* (behaviors and physical attributes patients and doctors can observe). In the process, shifts have occurred in the standard diagnostic system used in American psychiatry, and these shifts have caused strong scientific and heated political debate. The diagnostic system that has become the standard for American psychiatry is described in the American Psychiatric Association's *Diagnostic and Statistical Manual of Mental Disorders*. The third edition of this standard reference book, published in 1980, is usually referred to simply as *DSM-III*.

Diagnosis of Anxiety Disorders According to *DSM-III*

The chapter of *DSM-III* that deals with Anxiety Disorders is reproduced as the Appendix with permission of the American Psychiatric Association. In addition to descriptions of essential features of each mental disorder, *DSM-III* also provides information about associated features, age at onset, course of the disorder, range of impairment, complications, predisposing factors, prevalence (how common the disorder is), ratio of males to females, and differential diagnosis (that is, guidelines on how a doctor can differentiate between two disorders with similar symptoms when making a diagnosis). Much of this information is sketchy because the authors of *DSM-III* did not want to overstate what was known. *DSM-III* is used for diagnosis by 98 percent of American psychiatrists, but diagnostic thinking continues to evolve as new knowledge emerges. A revised version of the *Diagnostic and Statistical Manual (DSM-III-R)* is scheduled for release in 1987, and an entirely new edition *(DSM-IV)* will probably be published by the mid–1990s. Outside of the United States, some *DSM-III* concepts are questioned, and other diagnostic systems are in use, notably the *International Classification of Diseases* of the World Health Organization.

The Diagnostic Process

Even when patients have symptoms and signs that do not exactly satisfy criteria for a specific *DSM-III* diagnosis, they may receive that diagnosis. For example, a doctor might feel that a diagnosis of Agoraphobia with Panic Attacks (classified in *DSM-III* under the number 300.21) would be appropriate in someone with clear episodes of Panic Attack even though the panics occurred too infrequently to satisfy the *DSM-III* criteria for Panic Disorder (300.01). (The classification numbers are used merely as a way to identify various diagnoses in a simple and standardized way—for example, to indicate a diagnosis on an insurance form.)

Anxiety is the hallmark of Anxiety Disorders. In Panic Disorder without Agoraphobia and in Generalized Anxiety Disorder, anxiety is the main experience. In Phobic Disorders, Obsessive-Compulsive Disorders, and Post-Traumatic Stress Disorder, anxiety arises only as the person comes into contact with or thinks about particular situations.

The remainder of this chapter describes the various Anxiety Disorders and includes actual descriptions by people who are suffering from the disorders. We have decided to follow the organization of Anxiety Disorders contained in *DSM-III*, but we have added Blood-Injury, Illness and Dysmorphophobias, Social Skills Deficits, and Epidemic Anxiety, since they appear to us to be distinct disorders. In addition, in light of new knowledge, our own experience, and our professional opinions, we have amplified or modified *DSM-III* descriptions where we felt they were incomplete.

PHOBIC DISORDERS

Agoraphobia With and Without Panic Attacks

Agoraphobia is the most common and the most distressing phobic disorder seen in adults who come for treatment. The German psychiatrist Westphal first described Agoraphobia in 1871: There is the ''. . . impossibility of walking through certain streets or squares, or possibility of so doing only with resultant dread of anxiety.'' Westphal chose the term Agoraphobia carefully from the Greek word *agora,* which refers to marketplaces where people assemble, rather than "open spaces" as it is sometimes translated. *Phobia* means a persistent, unrealistic, and intense fear of an object or situation. People with Agoraphobia may fear crowds in theaters, churches, meeting halls, and marketplaces. They also may fear any situation in which they may feel stuck even if crowds are not present. There may be considerable differences between the things agoraphobics fear, but the common fear is of *feeling caught or trapped in some situation from which they cannot make a graceful and speedy exit to some place of safety.* Agoraphobics often fear the occurrence of panic, which might incapacitate them. Having a knowing and trusted friend or family member along who could take over if panic occurred may permit them to attempt and accomplish things they could not do on their own. Some, however, prefer to be alone so that they would not have to disclose their anxiety and reason for rapidly departing should panic occur.

Symptoms of panic include any of the following: feeling short of breath; palpitations; chest tightness or pain; choking or smothering sensations; dizziness or unsteady feelings; numbness and tingling of fingers, toes, or lips; feelings of unreality; hot and cold flashes; sweating; feelings of faintness; trembling or shaking; nausea; fear of vomiting or losing control of bladder or bowel; and fear of dying, going crazy, or doing something uncontrolled during an attack. Panic is described more fully on pages 49–53.

The situations in which agoraphobics feel trapped or caught vary widely, but some situations have a predictable character; it is this predictable character that often allows Agoraphobia to be properly diagnosed. Different agoraphobics may be frightened of church; sporting events; eating out; appointments with doctors, dentists, barbers, or hairdressers; driving on interstate highways; having to cross a lane of oncoming traffic while turning off of a road, even when it is actually safe to do so (these people might make three right turns rather than turn left once); taking a shower (what could these persons do if they panicked while they were naked and felt the urge to run out?); and so on. The common element in Agoraphobia is the fear of being caught or trapped in situations where help might not be available or escape to a self-defined haven might be difficult.

Agoraphobia and Panic

Experts disagree over the role panic attacks play in the onset and evolution of Agoraphobia. Some feel that panics are secondary, occurring in most or all agoraphobics when sufficiently exposed to agoraphobic situations (phobic or situational panic).

Other experts believe that panic attacks are usually the initiating events that eventually, in some people, lead to Agoraphobia. In this scenario, people are thought to respond to panic attacks by developing *anticipatory anxiety* about returning to situations in which panics occurred and, ultimately, by avoiding those settings (phobic avoidance). The end result, for some, is Agoraphobia.

In some agoraphobics, panics may have been present at the onset of their illness but no longer occur; in others, panic remains a consistent part of Agoraphobia; and in still others, there is no history of panic in the past or present. Finally, some people experience panic attacks without developing avoidance behaviors and Agoraphobia (see pages 49–53). The exact role that panic plays in the cause and persistence of Agoraphobia remains to be determined.

Poignant descriptions by sufferers of Agoraphobia illustrate common features and the dysfunction and distress that are experienced. That Agoraphobia is nothing new is shown by this description written by an American in 1890:

> The first noticeable symptoms . . . were extreme nervous irritability, sleeplessness, and loss of appetite. Any little excitement would throw me into a state of almost frenzy, so completely would I be overcome. Palpitation, spasmodic breathing, dilation of the eyes and nostrils, convulsive movements of the muscles, difficulty in articulation, etc., were the more prominent features. A sense of impending dangers seemed to descend, spoiling every pleasure, thwarting every ambition. The dread of sudden death which was at first marked, gradually subsided, giving way more to a feeling of dread— not of dying suddenly—but of doing so under peculiar circumstances or away from home. I became morbidly sensitive about being brought into close contact with any large number of people. Finding myself in the midst of a large gathering would inspire the feeling of terror . . . [which] could be relieved in but one way—by getting away from the spot as soon as possible. Acting on this impulse I have left churches, theaters, even funerals, simply because of an utter inability to control myself to stay. For 10 years I have not been to church, to the theater, to political gatherings or any form of popular meeting, except where I could remain in the background, with means of egress convenient. Even at my mother's funeral, when it would be supposed that everything else would be subordinated to the impulses of natural affection, I was utterly unable to bring myself to sit with the other members of the family in the front of the church. Not only has this unfortunate trait deprived me of an immense amount of pleasure and benefit, but is has also been a matter of considerable expense. More than once I

have got off a crowded train halfway to the station for which I was bound, merely from my inability to stand the jostling and confusion incident to the occasion. Times more than I can recall I have gone into restaurants or dining rooms, ordered a meal and left it untouched, impelled by my desire to escape the crowd. Times more than I recall I have bought tickets to theaters, concerts, fairs, or what-not, merely to give them away when the critical moment arrived and I realized the impossibility of my facing the throng with composure. To illustrate: I remember once going from Chicago to Omaha with my little boy. On entering the sleeper I found it crowded. I at once became ill-at-ease. As the train moved on I became more and more desperate, and finally . . . procure[d] a section by myself . . . [in] a stateroom . . . paying $10 extra for it. Had it been $100 and I had the money, I should have bought it without once counting the cost.

[A fear of open spaces] has been at times very pronounced. Many a time I have slunk in alleys instead of keeping on the broad streets, and often have walked long distances—perhaps a mile—to avoid crossing some pasture or open square, even when it was a matter of moment to me to save all the time possible. The dominating impulse is to always have something within reach to steady myself by in case of giddiness. This feeling is at times so strong that even when on a steamboat or a vessel, I cannot bear to look across any wide expanse of water, feeling almost impelled to jump in out of sheer desperation. . . . This malady . . . has throttled all ambition, and killed all personal pride, spoiled every pleasure. . . . Over this the will seems to have no control. At times buoyed up by stimulants or temporary excitement, I have faced situations which would ordinarily have filled me with extreme trepidation; but as a rule I have to yield or suffer the consequences. What those consequences would be, I do not know.

The severity of panic is often unrecognized even by neighbors and acquaintances if the sufferer is able to continue working. A distinguished English professor at the University of Wisconsin described his malady in a book published in 1928:

> The brief trips to Bonn filled me with a surging sense of the impossible and the fear . . . that could convert a half mile, or even five blocks from home, in terms of subjective need and cowardice, into an infinity of remoteness. . . . [I developed] a strange new phobia of water. In rowboat, canoe or launch I had for terror to hug the shore; I had always previously crossed the lake from point to point over [miles] . . . of open water. . . . I tried to master these fears by the elementary device of "try and try again" to no purpose. . . . Terror would drag me back, terror of being so far from safety. . . . The net result of this "cure" was [that] thereafter I found my normal rowing limit from shore reduced from 200 feet to 50. . . .
>
> [Later, after my wife's suicide,] the panics subsided into mere diffused dread . . . a relative relief . . . trying to fight back another seizure. . . . I have another seizure, I try to run it off. . . . I start a little walk down the street about a hundred feet from the house, I am compelled to rush back, in horror of being so far away . . . a hundred feet away . . . from home and security. I have never walked or ridden, alone or with others, as a normal man, since that day. . . . At times this emotional effect remains merely a diffuse state of terror, an intensity running the

whole scale from vague anxiety to intensest feel of
impending death; . . . I am in terror of the seizure of
terror, and I fear seizure at a given distance; there
are then perfectly rational subterrors lest I may
panic and make a public spectacle of myself,
or . . . actually collapse from nervous exhaustion as
soon as I get a certain distance from home—a
distance varying back and forth from yards to
miles. For the past 15 years I am overwhelmed
with the feeling of insecurity, or terror that I can't
hit back.

Agoraphobia appears to occur equally frequently in people of all social strata, economic means, education, race,
and religions. It is more frequent in individuals whose
family members suffer from depression or Anxiety Disorders and, perhaps, where alcohol abuse is present in the
family. About two-thirds of agoraphobics are women. Onset
may be abrupt or gradual and rarely follows a specific
severe traumatic event (two studies identified traumatic
events immediately preceding the onset of Agoraphobia in
only 3 to 8 percent of people). By contrast, smaller stressors
(stress-provoking factors) in the course of life's events were
reported twice as commonly by agoraphobics as by a control
population. However, increased numbers of stressors precede many other health events, including broken bones,
myocardial infarction, tuberculosis, depression, schizophrenia, and even pregnancy! Some agoraphobics point to a
seemingly trivial event as setting off Agoraphobia, even
though they experienced the same event many times before
without problem.

It has been observed in one Australian study that more
Agoraphobia begins in hot summer weather than in the
colder winter months. Perhaps agoraphobic individuals get
unusually anxious when they experience physiological changes

such as sweating and increased heart and breathing rates, which all increase in everyone during hot weather.

When spontaneous panics occur, they usually last from two to 10 minutes, rarely extending to a few hours. Phobic panics triggered by public situations are usually quickly switched off by the person escaping from those stiuations. After the panic dies down, the person often feels washed out or drained for some time.

Agoraphobic distress varies from day to day, sometimes for reasons people cannot discern and, at other times, in response to particular changes. Thus, most may prefer cloudy days but a few may prefer sunny days. Most may worry while streets are full of people as the result of stores being open, but a few may fret when streets are empty and stores are closed, which means that help would not be readily available if anxiety were great. Again, the degree of distress seems to depend on very individual interpretations of what will increase security and chances of help and what will decrease the risk of being "trapped" should the anxiety occur.

Anticipatory anxiety and spontaneous panic are often present in untreated agoraphobics. Hyperventilation and its consequences (see pages 79–83) may aggravate them. Depression can precede, follow, or occur independently of Agoraphobia, sometimes complicating diagnosis for the treating physician. Obsessive-compulsive symptoms sometimes occur in agoraphobics but usually are mild and seldom require specific treatment.

Observers have often remarked that a housebound agoraphobic was able to leave the house and function normally during an emergency and mistakenly concluded that the agoraphobic is merely lazy and shirking routine responsibilities. This observation and reasoning is incorrect. Everyday events, such as leaving the house or riding a bus, seem like emergencies to an agoraphobic, and no one can be expected to function for long in a state of constant emergency. Agoraphobia is a disorder associated with a high degree of personal distress and disability.

Agoraphobia can have a major impact on families, resulting in drastic shifts in roles and responsibilities. Nevertheless, careful studies have found that the spouses and children of agoraphobics are no different from the families of people who do not suffer from Agoraphobia. Agoraphobic women have the same number of contacts with friends and family as other women do, but they fear involvements in large social groups. They also do less shopping. Husbands of agoraphobic women work somewhat less after onset of Agoraphobia in order to spend more time with their wives. Clinicians sometimes speculate that Agoraphobia may keep a marriage going just as a couple may have a baby when they find themselves likely to split up. In rare cases, there are couples in whom the spouse does not wish the agoraphobic partner to become more independent again, but these are very uncommon. Most spouses are delighted when their partners lose their phobic shackles; regain their previous independence, family relationships, and responsibilities; and return to their preagoraphobic patterns of activity.

Sexual functioning of men and women before the start of Agoraphobia was the same as in people who never develop Agoraphobia. After Agoraphobia emerges, sexual dysfunction increases, more in women then in men: Only 60 percent of agoraphobic women described regular sexual enjoyment and orgasm, though 83 percent of agoraphobic men did.

Unlike simple phobics (see pages 43–45), agoraphobics may also experience general nonagoraphobic symptoms such as fatigue, tension, spontaneous panic, obsessions, and depression.

In careful studies, differences between agoraphobics and

nonagoraphobics have not been documented with regard to separation anxiety; marital status; social or economic class; and marital and sexual adjustment, dependency, or other personality characteristics *before* Agoraphobia begins. The limitations that are associated with Agoraphobia are often depressing, and the patient's self-esteem decreases and dependency increases *after* the Agoraphobia starts to become a handicap.

The typical age of onset of Agoraphobia is 18 to 35 years old; with a later age of onset, the likelihood of associated depression increases. The first sign of any phobia is anxiety in the situation that frightens the person. In an agoraphobic, this anxiety will be in a public situation. Agoraphobia may begin suddenly, gradually, or with outbreaks interspersed with periods that are free of distress. Agoraphobia may abate spontaneously but commonly persist for many years, running a course of fluctuating severity without totally disappearing. The onset of depression, being alone in an unfamiliar place, being far from home, and being in confining surroundings usually make Agoraphobia worse. The opposite circumstances or sedative (antianxiety) drugs temporarily lessen Agoraphobia.

Numerous biological differences between agoraphobic and nonagoraphobic groups have been reported in specialized laboratory tests. Whether these biological differences specifically result from Agoraphobia or whether they are common to other kinds of severe anxiety is unknown. None of the laboratory tests available today are useful in the routine care of people with Agoraphobia, and the diagnosis of Agoraphobia rests on obtaining a careful medical history and excluding other possible disorders.

Table 2 indicates the frequency of symptoms and worst fears experienced by agoraphobics, and Table 3 demonstrates the main effects of Agoraphobia on individuals' lives.

Table 2. Symptoms and Worst Fears During a Panic, as Listed by 100 Patients with Agoraphobia

Symptoms	%	Worst Fears	Listed as First Fear (%)	Listed as Second Fear (%)
Nervous and tense	93	Death	13	20
Dizzy or faint	83	Fainting/collapsing	38	16
Agitated	80	Heart attack	4	4
Palpitations	74	Becoming		
Weak legs	73	mentally ill	6	1
Trembling/shaking	72	Causing a scene	6	7
Feeling totally		Inability to get		
unable to cope	66	home/to place		
Stomach churning	65	of safety	6	26
Sweating/perspiring	65	Losing control		
Shortness of breath	59	(e.g., becoming		
Confused	58	hysterical)	7	9
Things not quite real	57	Other personal		
Loss of control	52	illness	10	7
Tightness/pressure in the head	43			
Difficulty with eyes (blurred vision, etc.)	36			
Feeling of becoming paralyzed	19			

Reproduced from *Fears, Phobias, and Rituals: An Interdisciplinary Perspective*, by I. M. Marks (copyright © 1986 Oxford University Press; reproduced by permission).

In summary, Agoraphobia is the most common phobic disorder for which people seek treatment. It is also the most disabling phobic disorder. Sufferers fear a variety of public situations and experience panic and other unpleasant sensations when they face the things they fear. Other phobics also experience panic and unpleasant situations when they face the things they fear. The chief differences are the type of phobic situation that evokes anxiety in agoraphobics—public places rather than dogs, dirt, spiders, or whatever—and the high frequency with which sufferers also have spontaneous panics and depression.

Table 3.   Main Effects of Agoraphobia on Subjects' Lives

112 Men	%	818 Women	%
Unable to work	42	Social restrictions	29
Lack of social contacts	29	Personal psychological	
Personal psychological		effect	23
effect	11	Marital disharmony	14
Marital disharmony	9	Unable to work	14
Travel restrictions	4	Travel restrictions	11
Guilt about children	2	Guilt about children	6

Reproduced from *Fears, Phobias, and Rituals: An Interdisciplinary Perspective*, by I. M. Marks (copyright © 1986 Oxford University Press; reproduced by permission).

Social Phobia

Social Phobia is a common phobic disorder seen in Anxiety Disorder clinics. It involves fears of embarrassment or humiliation in social situations in which a person must "perform" and may be under observation or scrutiny. A certain amount of "performance anxiety" may be experienced by most people, and some individuals claim that a slight degree of anxiety is even helpful in giving them an "edge" in social situations or when they are performing. Social

Phobia is performance anxiety that has passed well beyond the point of being helpful. Those with Social Phobia usually find face-to-face confrontations difficult and are likely to look away. It is interesting to note that a fear of two staring eyes is present in many birds and mammals.

Public speaking anxiety (sometimes called "stage fright") is probably the most common Social Phobia and affects even professional actors or musicians. Unlike other phobic disorders, which are most common among women, Social Phobia is almost as common in men as in women. A public speaker or performer fears that he or she might be embarrassed or even humiliated if a train of thought is lost, lines are forgotten, or a note is missed. Other common Social Phobias are of blushing (high-neck blouses or turtleneck sweaters are often worn in attempts to hide such reddening), eating or drinking with others (where embarrassment would result if anxiety caused a visible tremor or resulted in spilling soup or other liquid), writing (an excellent salesman didn't work for seven years because of fear that his hand might shake while signing a contract in front of a customer and that such shaking would be interpreted by the customer as a sign of dishonesty), and difficulty urinating or defecating in public bathrooms (more common in males standing before urinals, but both sexes may be troubled with embarrassment arising either from an inability to eliminate or from the sounds of elimination).

Many social phobics describe shyness from early childhood, but most shy children overcome their shyness and do not become socially phobic. Social Phobias usually begin after puberty with the peak of onset in the late teens and few beginning after age 30. Social Phobias usually increase over a period of months, plateau for months or years, and often decrease in severity in later life. They can, at times, persist for years at an intense level and cause considerable disabili-

ty. Social Phobias can cause great discomfort. One patient
described his problems as follows:

> My disorder is the fear of speaking in front of
> groups. This includes just stating my name at a
> conference and, occasionally, in small meetings
> that are likely to be tense or involve people I don't
> know that well.
>
> I was never too happy about speaking in front of
> classes in grammar school, although I remember
> participating in spelling bees and enjoying them.
> The first event I remember causing me great stress
> was when I was supposed to read a poem to the
> entire school during a pageant in the seventh grade.
> I pretended I was ill that day and didn't go to school.
>
> I can't remember any significant events in high
> school. I didn't like serious class presentations, but
> I don't think I avoided any. As an undergraduate, I
> had no problems until my junior year when the
> classes became smaller and presentations had to be
> made. I didn't skip any, but became very nervous
> before and during my presentations and usually
> talked in a monotone. Only once did I drink alco-
> hol to calm me down (two shots of liquor, which
> didn't help).
>
> Then the significant event occurred in my senior
> year. It was a seminar with 15 people, and I rarely
> spoke up all year. One time when I was daydreaming
> the professor asked me to tell the class about a
> project proposal I had submitted. I was surprised,
> my heart beat faster, and I tried to pull my thoughts
> together. My mind went blank for a second and I
> turned red (I blush easily in these circumstances). I
> then started thinking about the fact that I was now
> red and couldn't concentrate on the subject. The
> result was panic and the urge to flee, so I started
> coughing as if I were choking on something and

left the room. I felt awful and didn't know what to do. After one to two minutes, I was fairly composed and went back into the room. The professor, who was surprised by my departure, had started telling the class of my project. I came in and said in an airy way that I had swallowed my Life Saver candy, thanked the professor, and then proceeded to talk about my project. Apparently, they believed the Life Saver story. Since that time (eight years ago), I am very afraid of a repeat reaction that won't be accepted as well. While I am very happy that, at the time, I was able to recover from it and go back in, I now tend to focus only on the panic reaction and the flight.

The fear has varied in intensity depending on the events I face. Major speaking engagements are the worst, causing me great distress weeks in advance. Smaller meetings are somewhat okay, sometimes not, but I usually don't worry too much in advance. I do manage to speak in public sometimes, but at no small psychological expense. I have another public presentation coming up in three to four weeks and am already very nervous about it.

The major negative effect has been on my self-esteem, self-confidence, and job performance. While my supervisors and coworkers are very understanding, I feel I put unfair burdens on them as a result of my disorder since I avoid, as much as possible, speaking activities and groups where I may have to speak, even if only to introduce myself. I get a little depressed about my disorder, but not to any significant degree.

A woman patient described two social phobias as follows:

Some of my symptoms are lifelong. From earliest memory, I was shy and uncomfortable even going to children's parties. Through college, I did not like to walk into the campus snackshop alone unless I knew there was someone there I could sit with. In early years, I was bothered by what I would consider a normal amount of stage fright, which with more experience grew less in some situations. I have always been surprised to find myself nervous in some public situations which I had successfully handled many times before; it was as if I were "internally different," rather than the situation different. More recently, negative feedback from some persons in authority about my personality—"timid, unassertive, nervous in a presentation"—have made what always was and is a real but at least partially manageable problem an almost unmanageable one in some circumstances. The most serious consequences arise in formal presentations and meetings. I get very upset even in presentations to groups I talk and work with all the time. In meetings, even going around the table to introduce ourselves and tell what we do is unpleasant. I usually muddle through but have to struggle in these situations which should be low threat since I work with these people everyday. I am afraid that people will perceive that I have behavioral difficulties and these perceptions will be negatives for me and my career.

A symptom which is totally new and unacceptable to me in my work environment is that I began having trouble signing documents for some people in authority. I have no trouble signing under other circumstances. After trying a number of things on my own, I decided I could not go on wondering and worrying when the next document was coming through or delay indefinitely some presentations I need to make.

Another woman wrote of a common social fear in what is usually a joyful occasion:

A good friend from high school was married a few weeks ago. As much as I really wanted to go to the wedding, in fact I dreaded it whenever I thought about it all summer from the time I got the invitation. I use this as an example of how this fear gets in my way. When the time came for the wedding, I went without Valium [diazepam] or other drugs and had a very good time with almost none of the nervous feelings. Yet I had been dreading the wedding for weeks in advance. Sometimes I think I rehearsed this event enough before I went that the fear just played itself out. Also, I just felt good about myself generally and that might have had an effect on how relaxed and unfearful I was.

A woman with vomiting phobia wrote:

I am a female, 24 years old, married with no children, and am at present doing a postgraduate teacher-training year. Simply, I am terrified by vomiting—either vomiting myself or seeing, hearing, or even thinking about others vomiting. I don't know how common this phobia is—I have only met one other person who suffers from it—but I have always felt that, being fairly superficial, it might somehow be eradicable.

As to the exact nature of my phobia—I realize that vomiting is an activity which few must regard with delight, but I regard it not so much with dislike as with horror. When I was younger, seeing vomit or people vomiting did make me feel nauseated (which is probably normal), but gradually I came to feel more and more terror rather than nausea. I feel all the typical fear symptoms when confronted with "vomiters"—racing pulse, shock, feeling faint, desire to run or scream—and these may later give rise to hysteria, overall trembling, and diarrhea, especially if the "vomiter" is my husband whom I usually trust not to vomit under any circumstance.

The trouble with this phobia is it is so restricting—I like parties, but I daren't stay late at night when people might vomit. (This doesn't apply so much now that my friends and I are older and don't vomit much.) I get terrified travelling on subways and buses because of the times in the past that people have been sick in front of me—even in the daytime. I can't travel on planes or ships either without suffering agonies of anticipation—viewing each pale face as a "potential vomiter." I am unhappily very observant about nonverbal communication, posture, and expression—I can see that someone will vomit long before they do—or that they are drunk or dizzy or feeling unwell, which all produce the same terror in me.

As a teacher, and I suppose also as a potential parent, the fear of having to cope with children who are ill and need comfort and help is daily (or more usually nightly) a real threat to my peace of mind. I suppose I would cope if I had to, but in the past it has often taken weeks to recover from bad incidents of this kind, and as a teacher or a parent one cannot afford weeks—or hysteria or fainting. I'm worrying myself to bits and it gets worse rather than better as the years go on.

The other facet of my phobia is fear of vomiting myself. In fact I am physically incapable of vomiting as far as I can see. I haven't been sick since I was about 15 and that was an isolated occurrence amid many vomitless years. Nowadays when I "ought" to be sick, after too much drink or too much rich food—as soon as I feel sick all my muscles contract and relax in spasms and these spasms associated with painful stomach cramps alternate with relaxed moments for perhaps hours until whatever it is wears off. I know all this sounds very self-conscious and hypochondriacal, but I suspect this is merely the result of years of self-observation and "soul searching" coupled with a university education!

If called upon to do so, I could probably give numerous Freudian interpretations (and others) of both my symptoms and the reasons for them—on rereading this letter I can see a few glaring examples—but self-analysis never did help in this case!

Well, there it is. I would be extremely grateful if anyone had any ideas on how I might be helped—I realize that my problem is trivial compared with those of others, but it is very important to me so I had to try this last chance.

Social Phobia, while less common and less incapacitating than Agoraphobia, creates substantial social handicaps for those suffering from it. It is common in both men and women. Often occurring in people who were unusually shy as children, Social Phobia frequently emerges at the time greater social activity and involvement is necessary at school, work, and in relationships. Impending social obligations cause anticipatory anxiety and phobic avoidance and panic symptoms may also occur. Depression makes this phobia, as all Anxiety Disorders, worse. Behavioral treatments are effective for people with Social Phobia. Medication may also have a role to play for some sufferers.

Social Skills Deficits

Social Skills Deficits refer to the anxiety and difficulty some people have in forming superficial or intimate relationships when these are sought and desired. Other terms to describe the problem are social inadequacy, avoidant personality disorder, and extreme shyness. Social Phobias merge imperceptibly with Social Skills Deficits. No formal comparison between them has been published, but some insight may be gained by examining features of the latter.

The characteristics of 46 subjects with social dysfunction and associated anxiety were compared with those of other outpatients referred for behavior therapy in the Maudsley Hospital in London. Their social dysfunction was said to be "lifelong"; most (61 percent) reported having had no friends at school and recognized their problem in their teens. The problem largely manifested as a difficulty in initiating and maintaining social interaction and friendships, especially with new peers and members of the opposite sex. Social activities were few, apart from going to a bar where alcohol and the possibility of drinking in relative isolation reduced anxiety. They found it difficult to go to parties or dances. In social situations they feared ridicule or criticism, looking silly, losing control, or having a panic, and it was hard to talk about their feelings. Over 60 percent had had psychiatric treatment in the past, especially for depression (35 percent) and for the social dysfunction (22 percent). In another sample, in which students were the subjects, lack of assertion correlated with low self-esteem, interpersonal anxiety, fear of disapproval, and depression.

The average age of the individuals who sought help for Social Skills Deficits (34 years) was similar to that of other outpatients. Like social phobics they had a higher social class and education than other outpatients. Three-quarters were either living alone or with their parents. They were more often male and unmarried, 57 percent were virgin, and most of the remainder had difficulties in sexual performance. Many of the patients asked for sex therapy after social skills training made the possibility of intimate relationships more likely.

Interestingly, more of the men (but not women) with Social Skills Deficits were the first-born child or only child in their families. We might speculate whether older siblings are important as social role models for males. Among people with Obsessive-Compulsive Disorder, too, first-born males predominate.

In conclusion, social phobics have fears that are more limited to particular situations and more discrete in onset than the anxiety of those with Social Skills Deficits, which is more like a trait of shyness in extreme form. The two groups overlap; they fear some similar situations and include more subjects who are men and have higher social class and education than do other phobics.

Dysmorphophobia (Sometimes Called *Monosymptomatic Hypochondriasis*)

The fears and avoidance of most social phobics are different from those of people with *dysmorphophobia*, whose problem may also drive them into avoiding social situations and living the life of a recluse. Dysmorphophobia describes persistent complaints of some defect in a specific part of the body that is not noticeable to others; occasionally several parts of the body are involved. Sometimes the idea is so fixed that it amounts to a delusion (a firmly fixed false belief), and some people may exhibit other features of schizophrenia, suggesting that the primary problem is one of schizophrenia rather than something more akin to phobia. In other people, there is no evidence of schizophrenic disorder or other psychotic phenomena when observed over several years. Dysmorphophobics have no disturbance of body image as a whole, unlike people with anorexia nervosa who perceive themselves as overweight even while they are starving themselves (sometimes to death), or transsexuals who feel that their body is of the wrong sex and who may seek operations or medications to change their physical gender.

In contrast to social phobics, dysmorphophobics do not think that their anxiety is silly, nor do they feel much better when away from the social situations that they avoid; they are more preoccupied with a specific aspect of their body. Some cases of dysmorphophobia, however, are intermediate. Although exposure treatment (explained in Chapter 10) can be helpful for dysmorphophobics who avoid social situations, in our experience they usually refuse it; when they do accept treatment, improvement tends to be slow.

Dysmorphophobia usually first occurs in young adult life; many dysmorphophobics have always been shy. Their complaint may center on their fears that their body, limbs, penis, breasts, or parts of their face or body are misshapen or too large or small, or their fears of bad odors coming from their sweat or breath, or from their genitals or rectum. Sufferers worry that others comment adversely about their appearance or smell, and so they avoid company. They will try to conceal the body part about which they are self-conscious and may be unable to look others in the eye. Some avoid looking in a mirror because they become so upset by what they think they see, or wash themselves zealously to remove odor that in fact is imperceptible to anyone else.

Many dysmorphophobics ask plastic surgeons to correct the imagined stigma, but even after cosmetic surgery the anxiety remains. Problems other than the specific bodily preoccupation also persist afterwards. Among patients in one study who had a rhinoplasty (nose operation) 15 years earlier, more among those who had been operated on for strictly cosmetic reasons were severely neurotic or schizophrenic than among those who had operations for disease or injury. Depression, too, is common. In a dermatology clinic depression was more common among dysmorphophobics complaining of too little or too much hair or of skin blemishes than it was among patients with psoriasis or normal control subjects.

Just how Dysmorphophobia fits together with the disorders of Social Phobia, schizophrenia, and sometimes depression remains unclear. Treatment is difficult and trials of behavior therapy and antipsychotic and antidepressant medication are warranted based on present knowledge and experience.

Other Conditions Causing Social Avoidance

In schizophrenia, paranoid delusions may lead sufferers to shun company much as social phobics do, but the psychotic features usually indicate that the primary problem is schizophrenia. Similarly, people with Obsessive-Compulsive Disorders can become housebound for fear that contact with situations outside will trigger rituals; this latter feature makes it obvious that it is not a Social Phobia.

Simple Phobia

Simple Phobias are also called *specific phobias* because they involve specific phobic objects such as animals, insects, closed spaces, travel, heights, darkness, thunder, pointed objects, flowers, water, reptiles, etc. Some of these situations are also feared by agoraphobics, but their dread is of many objects and situations in contrast with the dread of one or a few objects in Simple Phobia. Animal phobias usually begin in childhood, when they are common in both sexes (see Table 1 on page 8). Most children outgrow their early phobias, and the few who remain phobic for animals into adult life are usually women. Except for their particular fear, people with Simple Phobia are usually emotionally intact and unlikely to announce or display their fear unless confronted with the specific cause of their anxiety. If they have to go somewhere, they will seek assurance that their phobic object is not present and, if they cannot be reassured, may avoid the situation.

Flying phobia is common; 10 percent of the population will not fly at all, while an additional 20 percent experience substantial anxiety sometimes leading to panic attacks if they do fly. Many people use alcohol or other drugs to help allay their anxiety before they board airplanes. Erica Jong caught the flying phobic's fear in her best selling novel, *Fear of Flying:*

> My fingers (and toes) turn to ice, my stomach leaps upward into my ribcage, the temperature in the tip of my nose drops to the same level as the temperature in my fingers. . . . I happen to be convinced that only my own concentration . . . keeps this bird aloft. . . . I congratulate myself on every successful takeoff but not too enthusiastically because it's also part of my personal religion that the minute you grow overconfident and really relax about the flight, the plane crashes instantly. . . .

Fears of insects or animals are often tolerated and left untreated until the phobic encounters the feared situation repeatedly. One patient described her fear of spiders as follows:

> When I was around four or five years old I sudden-
> ly became frightened of spiders and have been
> constantly afraid of them ever since. I don't recall
> any specific incident that brought on my fear and
> my mother doesn't remember that I was bitten by a
> spider or anything like that. My fear is that a spider
> will get on me. Generally, it's not much of a
> problem since I know where spiders hang out and
> stay away from those places. I am more uncomfort-
> able in warm weather when there are more spiders.
>   Recently, we bought a piece of land in the
> country where we plan to build our home. It's
> covered with tall grass and I just can't go there
> because I'm afraid I'll run into a spider web or a
> spider. I also tend to avoid dark places where I'd
> have trouble seeing spiders and places I think they
> might be lurking, such as curtains. The reason I
> came for treatment is that I've got to get over this
> fear if we're going to build our house. Today was
> one of the worst experiences I have had. I was in
> the bathroom and a spider was in the doorway. I
> couldn't get out of the bathroom and started shak-
> ing, crying, and screaming at the spider. I was
> stuck there for about 10 to 15 minutes until my
> husband came home and killed the spider. I was
> pretty shook up the rest of the day.

Simple phobics are seldom seen in Anxiety Disorder clinics because, unlike agoraphobics and social phobics, their narrow problem seldom interferes with functioning. Of the few who seek help, many are easily treated with straight-forward exposure therapy (see Chapter 6).

Blood-Injury Phobia

People with *Blood-Injury Phobia* are unusual in that many of them actually faint if confronted with blood or if exposed to pain through inadvertent injury, injections, dental work, or sometimes even when they hear talk of blood or injury to others. In contrast, agoraphobics often fear fainting but virtually never actually faint; hyperventilation causes or aggravates their fear of fainting. The actual fainting of blood-injury phobics is from stimulation of the vagus nerve; this slows the heart so much that not enough blood reaches the brain if they are sitting or standing. If they faint and fall down, or lie down before they faint, consciousness is rapidly regained because even a very slow heart rate will pump enough blood to the brain if it is not having to work against the force of gravity encountered in an upright position. Heart rate rapidly returns to normal after people faint from Blood-Injury Phobia.

People with Blood-Injury Phobia are usually quite physically and psychologically well in other regards. We are all familiar with the cliché of the strapping military inductee who is ready to fight and, if necessary, die for his country but who faints when given an injection. In addition to the embarrassment people with this problem experience, and their tendency to avoid medical care, fainting is neither fun nor safe, so treatment is important.

One man with a needle phobia described his problem:

> I'm afraid to have blood tests because every time they put a needle in my arm I faint. This is the dumbest thing because I am not afraid of anything else I can recognize. But every time I've had blood drawn from the time I was 12 [he is now 32], I fainted or sure felt like I was going to. The only

times I haven't fainted are when I've told the
person about my problem and they had me lie
down before they put the needle in my arm. Although I am healthy and very fit, this problem still
worries me because I never know when I may need
medical care. I'm also embarrassed that I can't do
such a simple thing when most people can. My
mother also has this trouble, and we've both taken
a fair amount of teasing about it.

This patient was treated with four sessions of exposure to
blood drawing in a hospital blood-drawing station. First, he
was simply asked to lie on a couch to lessen the chance of
fainting and watch other patients having blood drawn. Then
a needle and syringe were brought close to his arm. His
pulse was monitored and as long as it did not fall, the
needle was brought closer. At the end of the session he was
given a needle and syringe and tube of blood to take home
and carry in his pocket.

During the second session, blood was actually drawn with
him lying flat on his back and not looking at the needle. His
heart rate did not fall and he didn't faint but he still wanted
to be able to have blood drawn in a sitting position. During
the third and fourth sessions, he progressed steadily to a full
sitting position and direct observation of the blood drawing
procedure. During the last session, blood was drawn four
times with no fall in pulse rate and no feelings of faintness.

Illness Phobias

Fears of illnesses are familiar to almost everyone. Medical students routinely "come down with" many of the
diseases they study, miraculously recovering only when they
read of a new malady during their studies.

Illness phobics, however, develop a persistent and severe fear of contracting, suffering from, and ultimately dying of cancer, heart disease, venereal disease, or any other illness. Endless worry leads to self-examination, repeated requests for evaluation and reassurances from physicians, and avoidance of situations that may remind the person of the dread disease. Sometimes illness fears emerge in the context of depression. Illness Phobia differs from hypochondriasis because the hypochondriac fears many diseases while the illness phobic is preoccupied with a single disorder.

One illness phobic described her fears as follows:

> I have a terrible fear of contracting cancer. Somehow, I've got the idea that if I get near people who have cancer I'll get it. This leads me to avoid hospitals, nursing homes, friends who I know have cancer, and—especially—doctors. I haven't been to see a doctor for 12 years although I'm pretty sure I have high blood pressure, and I worry that I might be developing a cancer that could be found if I could only go for a physical examination.
>
> I'm 48 years old and, in one form or another, I've always been afraid of illness. When I was younger, I worried about the risk of polio to the point that I wouldn't go swimming at all in the community pool even when there hadn't been any reports of polio. My parents were very upset with me and pushed me to do things other children did, and I gradually got over my fear of polio. Next came a fear of pneumonia even though no one in our family had ever had pneumonia. I had read in the newspaper that old people were dying of pneumonia during a flu epidemic. I worried about pneumonia for almost 10 years until I finally got it and recovered promptly with antibiotic treatment. I don't know where the fear of cancer began but I have

worried about all kinds from brain cancer to kidney cancer to breast cancer to cancer of the womb.

I've never followed any particular rituals to disinfect myself or anything like that and I don't wash any more than anyone else in my family. The only thing I try to do is avoid situations where I think I might be exposed to cancer. This causes me to be always on guard and any time I even drive past a hospital, I feel anxious.

This problem has been a real source of distress for me and my family. I can't go with them lots of places and I feel very guilty for letting my friends down when they fall ill and I can't visit them in the hospital. It's so bad I won't even go to a funeral of someone who has died of cancer.

ANXIETY STATES

Panic Disorder

Panic Disorder is characterized by repeated panic or anxiety that usually occurs spontaneously or unpredictably: "out of the blue... without warning." Mild situational (phobic) panic may be present, but usually there is no consistent avoidance. For some reason, when panics happen to occur in public places, sufferers tend to ascribe the panics to being in those places, and they come to avoid public places in the disorder called Agoraphobia with Panic Attacks. Avoidance does not occur when panics strike the sufferer in other places, like in bed or in a forest—few if any agoraphobics avoid beds and forests.

Panic is characterized by the sudden onset of symptoms like shortness of breath; palpitations; chest pain or discomfort; choking or smothering sensations; dizziness, vertigo, or unsteady feelings; feelings of unreality; paresthesias (usually numbness and tingling in the hands, feet, or around the lips); hot and cold flashes; sweating; faintness; trembling or shaking; and fear of dying, going crazy, or doing something uncontrolled during an attack. Each of these symptoms can be caused by hyperventilation. Three panics within a three-week period are required to strictly satisfy the requirements for the *DSM-III* diagnosis of Panic Disorder, but people with classic symptoms who fail to experience three panics in such a short time may also suffer from a form of Panic Disorder.

Women are somewhat more likely than men to suffer from Panic Disorder. Onset usually occurs in late adolescence or early adult life but may begin somewhat earlier or later. Sometimes people suffer a Panic Disorder which lasts for a short period never to recur; others experience several series of panics separated by panic-free intervals, and a few develop a chronic disorder with frequent panics. Some people use alcohol in an attempt to prevent panics, which is ineffective and may lead to the complications associated with alcohol abuse.

One woman described her Panic Disorder as follows:

> My panics, as I've learned to call them, began at a time when life was very busy but also very good. I had gotten a promotion with a sizeable increase in pay and was on top of the world because I was finally doing what I had always wanted to do and knew I could do it very well. I was getting lots of compliments on my productivity and was taking some work home with me. I was drinking more coffee to keep me functioning at my highest level, and probably got up to six or eight cups a day. All in all, it was a great time in every way and my

family knew how pleased I was, and some of my success seemed to inspire them to do better too.

The first attack (I'll never forget it) occurred when I was sitting in the audience at my son's kindergarten "graduation" ceremony. That was three years ago when I was 26. Suddenly, I felt hot and as though I couldn't breathe. My heart was racing and I started to sweat and tremble and I was sure I was going to faint. Then my fingers started to feel numb and tingly and things seemed unreal. It was so bad I wondered if I was dying and asked my husband to take me to the emergency room. By the time we got there (about 10 minutes) the worst of the attack was over and I just felt washed out. The doctor checked me over very thoroughly but could find nothing wrong and said he thought I had had an anxiety attack. He told me not to worry about it because it wasn't dangerous. I tried not to worry but my mind kept saying that anything that extreme had to be dangerous.

The next attack occurred two days later when I was waiting in the checkout line at the grocery store. It wasn't quite as bad as the first one or maybe I just had an idea what it was. At any rate, I just pulled my cart out of the line and found a place to sit down until it passed. Even though I felt drained, I also felt pretty good that I hadn't lost control. I began to look for causes of the attacks in the two places I had been and came to the conclusion that the only common feature was that I was sort of stuck in both places and couldn't get up and get away without making a commotion.

The third attack woke me from sleep. After this attack I went to see my regular doctor who again examined me carefully and called the problem "panic attacks." He suggested I cut down my coffee intake, which I did quite easily. The fourth attack occurred at work at a time when everything was going perfectly. After this, I realized that if I tried to avoid all the situations where I was having panic attacks, I wouldn't be able to go anywhere with my family, go to work, or even sleep in my own bed! I decided whatever else happened, I'd have to tough these things out. That was three years ago. I've continued to have panic attacks about once every six months, and I'm darned if I can figure out anything specific that brings them on. I've tried exercising and sleeping more, and that certainly made me feel better in general and seemed to improve my mood, but I still have these attacks once every six months or so.

People with Panic Disorder often seek evaluation and treatment from general physicians because they are understandably frightened that they may suffer from a medical malady. By the time they reach a physician, the panic has usually disappeared and the physician can find nothing physically wrong. In the emergency room, a diagnosis of "acute hyperventilation syndrome" is often made, which may initially be gratifying to both doctor and patient but which does little or nothing to ensure a more definitive diagnosis and effective long-term treatment. The patient may feel chagrined that he or she has been alarmed about nothing but leave reassured by a careful examination. When the next panic occurs, help is often sought again, either from the same or another physician. One study found that patients with Panic Disorder had seen an average of 10 physicians before the disorder was finally diagnosed. General anxiety may occur between panics, as may some anticipatory anxiety and avoidance, although if the latter become pronounced, a diagnosis of Agoraphobia with Panic Attacks is made.

Generalized Anxiety Disorder

Generalized Anxiety Disorder is diagnosed when anxiety persists for at least a month but is not accompanied by the specific symptoms that characterize other Anxiety Disorders. Thus, one would not diagnose Generalized Anxiety Disorder in the presence of pronounced phobias, panic, obsessions, or compulsions. If the anxiety is caused by a medical disorder such as asthma, anemia, or hyperthyroidism, or by a mental disorder such as depression, the diagnosis of Generalized Anxiety Disorder is not made. Major symptoms include muscle tension, hyperactivity of many body functions (heart beat, breathing, stomach, bowels, and bladder), apprehension about an unrecognizable fear, and excessive vigilance.

People with Generalized Anxiety Disorder often complain of mild depressive symptoms and may abuse alcohol or sedative drugs to quell their anxiety. While distress may be substantial, impairment of important functioning is usually mild.

Obsessive-Compulsive Disorder

Many perfectly normal people are very tidy, clean, punctual, and diligent. Such traits can be a great help in their work and everyday living and certainly do not amount to a disorder. In the great majority of people, such traits never become excessive. In a few, however, the habits may increase to the point where they handicap the person's life because they come to involve hour after hour of tidying, cleaning, or checking. At that point, the problem has become an Obsessive-Compulsive Disorder. Many a case of Obsessive-Compulsive Disorder, however, begins in some people who have been untidy, messy, and unpunctual all their lives.

Obsessions are repeated, unwanted, or even repugnant ideas or thoughts or ruminations or impulses (urges) that intrude upon a person's consciousness. Obsessions may be fleeting and focused on a single subject or (as is common in individuals who seek treatment) persistent and involve numerous topics.

Compulsive rituals are repeated senseless behaviors usually performed against one's will. Rituals most frequently involve cleaning, avoiding, checking, and repeating in amounts above what an average person would do. Ritualizers usually become anxious if they are prevented from carrying out their accustomed rituals. Children and those who have ritualized for years may not be able to resist carrying out their rituals. Rituals are generally preceded by obsessive thoughts, but obsessive thoughts need not be followed by rituals. There are some individuals who are troubled only by obsessive thinking, and apart from the thinking itself being carried out ritualistically, there may be no actual rituals.

At times obsessions arise in the context of depression or schizophrenia, and it is important to recognize these disorders so that treatment can be directed at these primary causes of the obsessions. Treatments for schizophrenia are largely ineffective for Obsessive-Compulsive Disorder, and vice versa.

There are similarities between Obsessive-Compulsive Disorder and phobias. People feel anxious during obsessions and rituals and may avoid situations that stimulate them.

However, Obsessive-Compulsive Disorder may be differentiated from phobic disorders on at least three grounds:

1. Obsessive-compulsives are less worried about confronting a feared object, other than the price they will pay in hours or even days of obsessing and ritualizing after having contacted the object. For example, a phobic who is frightened of subways would avoid them at all cost, whereas an obsessive-compulsive who is apprehensive about contamination on subways might travel on them if able to perform a cleaning ritual afterward. As another example, a man with a fear of ringworm infection might avoid contact with children in the compulsive belief that they are a source of infection. He would be uncomfortable entering a barbershop in which children's hair had been cut a month before, but he might do so nevertheless if he knew that he could perform his cleaning ritual afterward.

2. The beliefs of obsessive-compulsives about the things that make them uncomfortable are often more complex than those of phobics. Someone who is afraid that she may confess a crime that she has not committed can imagine hundreds of ways, some of them quite bizarre, in which she might make such disclosures. Slight shifts in the way situations are preceived can have a major effect on an obsessive-compulsive's behavior. Thus, the person fearing ringworm infection from children would not enter a barbershop where children had been served even months before, but if told that children had never been served in a shop, he would enter with comfort.

3. When forced to confront the thing they fear, the reaction of obsessive-compulsives may be one of discomfort or disgust instead of or in addition to the obvious fear or panic that most phobics exhibit, although anxiety is still the usual reaction in obsessive-compulsives.

We can divide Obsessive-Compulsive Disorder into three components: *compulsive rituals*, *obsessions*, and *slowness*.

Compulsive Rituals

Many classifications of rituals can be given. What follows is based on our experience, including a survey of 45 cases seen at the Maudsley Hospital in London. Since some patients had more than one ritual, percentages (which are listed after the type of ritual) total more than 100.

Cleaning (51 percent). Women are affected by the obsessive cleaning ritual more often than men. Contact with real or imagined dirt or germs, or simply uncertainty about contact, may lead to hours of washing and cleaning. One of our patients showered for 33 consecutive hours, long after the hot water was gone! Urination, defecation, and any manner of self-defined "dirt" or germs can set off cleaning rituals of the body and surroundings.

Repeating (40 percent). When repeating is the obsessive ritual, some comfort is obtained only after the ritual is performed a certain number of times. For example, a man we treated had to repeat his brother's name three times (or some multiple of three times) each time he thought of him, in an attempt to ward off injury and illness in his brother. Though realizing, at one level, how unrealistic his fears and rituals were in the face of his brother's normal health, he initially became very uncomfortable on refraining from performing this ritual.

Completing (11 percent). The completing ritual is a subtype of repeating. People with this ritual feel that they must complete an action correctly. This often involves an often complicated sequence of steps that must be started again if they are interrupted or deviate ever so slightly from their accustomed pattern. There is obviously some overlap with the repeating ritual described above. Putting on clothing in the ''correct'' sequence or completing one's personal grooming in a particular and consistent manner, such as by combing the hair or brushing the teeth according to a rigidly specific and unvarying routine, are examples of completing rituals.

Checking (38 percent). Men are slightly more likely than women to display the compulsive ritual of checking. Doors and windows will be locked and relocked (sometimes so repetitively that the key or the lock is quickly worn out); electric switches and gas and water taps are turned off again and again even though they are visibly shut off; knives are locked away so they will not tempt the person to stab someone; and driving routes are retraced in search of victims who may have been run over or signs of accidents in which the person may have been involved.

Being meticulous (9 percent). A person with the compulsive ritual of being meticulous requires that things must be in their proper place. Any sort of deviation disrupts that person's progress. Arranging things on a desk or in a room according to an exact pattern is a common meticulous ritual.

Hoarding (percentage unknown). Hoarding is a less common but dramatic ritual. Here there is little concern with cleanliness or meticulousness; in fact, hoarders will collect all manner of things that they will never use and spend hours sorting and stacking them. Food scraps, newspaper, junk mail, and old clothing may accumulate to the

point that rooms are filled and fire hazards exist because
exits are blocked. Thoughts of giving up part of the hoarded
material may provoke great anxiety.

Avoiding (51 percent). The avoiding ritual is more common in women, perhaps because of its association with
cleaning rituals. Successful avoidance may protect the person against hours of ritualistic cleaning. Doubts whether avoidance had been successful may lead to ritualizing despite the
attempts at avoidance. Not just cleaning ritualizers are likely
to use the avoiding ritual, however. One woman's discomfort
with chocolate led her to avoid anything remotely related to
that substance, including anything merely colored brown.

Obsessions

Obsessions are unwanted repetitive thoughts, ideas, or
impulses that occur in the same pattern and intrude against
the person's will in spite of all attempts to block or forget
them. Common obsessions involve bringing harm or injury
to others or violating social norms, such as swearing or
making unacceptable sexual advances in public. While compulsive rituals are almost always preceded by obsessive
thoughts, some people have obsessive ruminations but do
not ritualize. Obsessive ruminations may involve religious
and philosophical concepts which are endlessly pondered in
an indecisive, despairing fashion.

Slowness

This disabling but uncommon problem is seen mainly in
men and is presently difficult to treat. It is interesting to note

that slowness does not affect all activities so that the person may be able to dress, talk, and play tennis at a normal rate but take an hour to clean a tabletop, moving either in slow motion or with long pauses between movements. Most such individuals report that their pauses between movements are for mental checking.

Obsessive-Compulsive Case Histories

One patient described her obsessions and compulsive rituals as follows:

> My disorder began around age 21, in 1975. It has been constantly present in various forms since then. The onset was gradual and I have never been completely free of it. I was a new R.N. [registered nurse] working at a hospital and not very confident. Every so often I would be afraid I contaminated a needle or IV, but I wasn't sure.
>
> I changed jobs in 1976. I left because I was doubting myself constantly in my nursing tasks. I would aspirate two or three times, afraid I hit a blood vessel while giving an injection. It would take me very long to clean proctoscopes after assisting in the procedure. I would throw things away (at one point a whole tube of KY jelly) because of fear of contamination. I would go from one doctor to another asking many questions regarding germs and air bubbles in syringes and what was safe. At this point I didn't have the feeling that I was constantly dirty or contaminating things at home—that came later.
>
> I left the clinic and worked for an insurance company in 1976–77 as a claims adjuster. That was fine until I started to check claims over and over to

see if I had coded them right. I felt guilty, and I do to this day, about my not working to my fullest and daydreaming a lot of the days away.

At this time my worst obsessions and compulsions started. I became unsure of whether I was clean enough when I went to the bathroom. I started obsessing and felt I had killed someone. I had trouble doing the wash—not knowing if I put soap in the machine. I had the feeling it was stool [feces] instead. I feel ashamed or guilty having such grotesque thoughts.

A young man described the start of his disorder as follows:

One of my aunts died in December 1978—I wasn't upset or sad. I had plans to buy a record album, but I delayed this for some time (a couple of weeks) because it seemed "inappropriate." This period continued to be extended up to the summer. Between this summer and the December before it, I was making specific prayers concerning my aunt. I also had to decide whether or not to draw pictures and submit them to my high school newspaper and put this decision "on hold" until the summer. Before this situation happened, I'd pray for a long time (maybe 15 minutes) with no problems at all. I did this because I enjoyed it and there was no specific length to what I'd pray about, but by the end of this summer of '79 the prayers had become obligatory and long. At this time I started to "put off" my prayers for later in the evening because they took so long. By fall of '79 I wouldn't let myself draw, run in school, or try out for the soccer team or listen to the radio. My life was filled with prayers and rituals. The prayers were long and for various purposes. I used to pray with no trouble.

I'm sure that no one else in my family did anything but one short prayer before bed. There were set things to pray for, but this varied over time. In addition I would repeat things like opening and closing a door. The worst time was in January '80. I received a bad grade on my report card and forced myself to do more school work. The price was to do a prayer before starting each subject. I finally saw that this wasn't going to end if I didn't do something soon.

But in the summer of 1980, I read something in the Bible that I interpreted incorrectly. I thought it meant that I had to keep blood off my hands (from mosquitoes or pimples for instance), so I washed my hands very much, especially after going to the bathroom. I stopped washing my hands when my parents found out about it during that summer.

From this point until November 1983, there was a very easy period. There were only a few small irritating things. For instance, checking to see that I didn't skip a page in a book or solve the wrong problem from a textbook.

In November or early December 1983, I started to think too hard on certain matters. I had a tutor for computers whom I thought was lonely. I started to think that if I didn't give her enough attention she might kill herself. While studying for my last exam in mid-December, I had a thought that seemed homosexual. I am positively sure that I'm not homosexual. When I didn't come up with a satisfying rationalization, I couldn't get back to studying. I wasted the rest of my study time thinking about the thought. When I got home I went over the thought some more, but still no reasoning was satisfactory. When I tried to just forget it, an overwhelming and horrible feeling engulfed my spine, I just had to come up with some "logical solution." I went over this issue ferociously for about two weeks. But soon after the issue ended another one started. I wasn't sure if I ruined my fasting for church. I went over this issue just as I did with the previous one (also for about two weeks). Then I drove my brother to a store. When he was through, I started to back out of my parking stall in the parking lot. The rear window was fogged up. From out of nowhere a man stepped into view and earlier on there was a group of kids playing in the parking lot. As I drove away I thought that maybe I didn't see a kid and ran over him. Later on I was sure I didn't hit the man, but I kept having doubts about the kids. My father even took me to the police station to check the accident records. The policeman said all was clear but it still bothered me. Every time I drove, I had to at least look, double check my driving actions in my mind. There were times when I'd drive back and check to see if there was a wreck or injured people.

Obsessive-Compulsive Disorder ranges from a mild problem, inconveniencing the individual only slightly and requiring no treatment, to one of the most severe and incapacitating psychiatric disorders known, lasting a lifetime. When severe, it is all the more distressing for patients and their doctors because patients are usually aware of the unreasonableness of their obsessions and the impracticality and incompleteness of their rituals as a solution for their anxiety. Fortunately, treatment is usually effective in Obsessive-Compulsive Disorder.

EPIDEMIC ANXIETY (MASS HYSTERIA)

Epidemic Anxiety, a quite common phenomenon, is not recognized in *DSM-III,* although an article published in the July 1985 issue of the *American Journal of Psychiatry* identifies more than 180 published reports of Epidemic Anxiety. From time to time brief epidemics of acute anxiety affect different communities. The epidemics last only a few days, and the persons affected recover without any lasting effects. Commonly, factors associated with the onset of anxiety can be identified, and the particular anxiety which appears may be culturally determined.

Most well known are the epidemics of fainting and anxiety about fainting that most often occur in girls' schools. A typical and well-documented fainting epidemic occurred in Blackburn, England in 1965. Precipitating circumstances included an epidemic of polio earlier in the year and, immediately before the epidemic, a ceremony was delayed for three hours while the girls waited standing in formation. Twenty of the 500 students felt faint and had to lie down. Fainting became a popular topic of discussion the next day, and at the school assembly one girl fainted and three others announced their dizziness. During the next two class periods, more girls complained of feeling faint and were excused to sit on chairs in the school corridor. To prevent falling from their chairs in the event of a faint, they were instructed to lie on the floor, where they were in full view of their classmates at change of class time. Cases multiplied and the epidemic was on. Each time the children assembled, more cases appeared. In the end, two-thirds of the 500 girls were affected, and more than 100 required hospital care. Many had repeated episodes of fainting. Girls became excited and fearful of fainting, which led to hyperventilation and its common symptoms of feeling faint (but not actually fainting), dizziness, numbness, and tingling of the fingers and toes and lips. Prolonged overbreathing led to tetany (a reversible kind of muscle spasm caused by a decreased calcium level in the blood). By the 12th day of the epidemic, the causes were identified and proper management prevented further spread of the problem.

Females are not the only victims of Epidemic Anxiety. A few months after an outbreak of swine fever and widely publicized inoculation of pigs to control the outbreak in Singapore, a few cases of Koro appeared. This curious anxiety is seen in Malaya and southern China and involves males who fear that the penis is shrinking into their abdomen. Elaborate and ingenious steps are taken to prevent this result. In Singapore, rumors spread that Koro could be caused by eating pork from infected or inoculated pigs. In the days that followed, nearly 100 cases of Koro per day were reported at hospitals, and many other people consulted their general practitioners. When the epidemic was at its height, experts explained the psychological nature of Koro on radio and television. Koro cases dropped sharply the next day, and the epidemic soon ended.

POST-TRAUMATIC STRESS DISORDER

Post-Traumatic Stress Disorder (sometimes called *traumatic neurosis* or *traumatic phobia*) occurs in the wake of a severe and unusual physical or psychological trauma. While some individuals are more resistant to the effects of trauma, almost everyone has a breaking point. Even the most robust of persons may break down if the trauma and injury are severe enough. When a person has had many traumatic blows—as in prolonged combat, torture, or incarceration in a concentration camp—the likelihood of Post-Traumatic Stress Disorder increases. If the individual has been physically injured—and, particularly, if there has been injury to the brain or spinal cord—the severity of Post-Traumatic Stress Disorder rises. Willful abuse from another human, or even witnessing such abuse, appears particularly likely to bring about the disorder. Absence of social and other supports seems to predispose individuals to the development of a more severe and longer lasting Post-Traumatic Stress Disorder. For example, a distressing aspect of the devastating flood disaster in Buffalo Creek, West Virginia, was that—in addition to the deaths of friends and family members—homes and other familiar landmarks simply disappeared. This abrupt loss of social support and community identity significantly contributed to the trauma experienced by the survivors.

The effect of trauma seems to be worse when the disaster is unexpected. Many soldiers endure prolonged and brutal combat, witness atrocities, and suffer wounds without developing Post-Traumatic Stress Disorder. By contrast, four years after the Chowchilla, California, kidnapping—in which schoolchildren were taken from their school bus and were subsequently buried alive in a truck—all of the children exhibited post-traumatic after-effects. Soldiers expect to encounter a certain amount of violence; children riding a school bus do not. An event that results in a sudden loss of confidence and trust in the way the world works and the way life should proceed may bring on a traumatic stress disorder.

Soldiers in combat, nonetheless, have long been recognized as being at risk of developing traumatic disorders. Freud and his disciples wrote about the traumatic neuroses of World War I, other researchers described them in World War II veterans, and there is a growing awareness of the frequency with which Vietnam veterans continue to suffer emotional repercussions of their combat duty, although not all of it is Post-Traumatic Stress disorder. In Vietnam, the tour of duty was specified in advance, but the policy of rotating individuals rather than units to comply with the specified length of the combat tour reduced unit cohesion and the support individuals could obtain from their comrades. The Post-Traumatic Stress Disorder experienced by Vietnam veterans is probably similar to that of soldiers in earlier wars.

The Israelis have most recently studied the effects of combat on the development of Post-Traumatic Stress Disorder, or "battle shock" as they describe it. In the 1973 Yom Kippur War, for every 10 nonfatal medical or wound casualties, another 30 soldiers became battle shock casualties. Israel learned from earlier American military medical experience and developed improved procedures for managing combat stress casualties. Israel was able to reduce the ratio to 23 battle shock casualties for every 100 nonfatal illness or wound casualties in the June to December 1982 Lebanon War. Post-Traumatic Stress Disorder and its management are of growing interest to the military of most countries, since soldiers with this disorder are a rapidly recoverable combat manpower resource. If treated close to their units, over two-thirds of soldiers with combat stress symptoms can recover and return to their units as effective combat soldiers within 24 to 72 hours. It is interesting to note that, of the Israeli soldiers who returned to combat in 1973, only 1 percent subsequently suffered a recurrence of acute combat stress symptoms during the campaign in Lebanon.

Description of Post-Traumatic Stress Disorder

After being subjected to some trauma that is outside the range of common human experience, susceptible individuals may develop the constellation of symptoms and signs we call Post-Traumatic Stress Disorder. They reexperience the trauma in the form of unpleasant, recurrent memories or flashbacks or nightmares. Rarely, there may be dissociative states of consciousness (a temporary "disconnection from reality") that last from a few seconds to hours or occasionally days, in which the affected person may act as though the traumatic event is recurring. People with Post-Traumatic Stress Disorder describe, and others observe, a decreased interest in and involvement with people and previously pleasant activities. This is sometimes called "emotional anesthesia" or "psychic numbing."

Anxiety and depression are common among people with Post-Traumatic Stress Disorder. The person may become excessively alert, startle with little or no provocation, and report sleep disturbance. Complaints of poor memory and difficulty in concentrating or following through on tasks may be expressed. Those who survive a disaster in which others died may feel guilty about continuing to live or about the things they did in order to survive. Any new situations which remind the person of the traumatic experience may revive or intensify remaining symptoms and are usually consciously avoided. When the person is required to reenter such situations, anxiety may turn into panic.

Post-Traumatic Stress Disorder follows an instance of exceptional trauma. Everyday problems are excluded as causes, such as death of a loved one, illness, family conflict, or ordinary business reversals. Trauma may occur in groups (concentration camps, combat, natural disasters) or

alone (rape, severe automobile accident). It may involve
intentional human abuse (concentration camps, combat, kidnapping, torture) or severe accidental disasters (airplane
crashes, fires, collapse of a building or a bridge) or even
natural disasters (tornadoes, floods, earthquakes). Some people may develop a phobia related to an accident as in the
following case:

> I had been driving trucks for more than 10 years and
> was darn good at it. I only went off the road once,
> when a car pulled in front of me and I didn't want
> to hit it.
>
> My big accident happened in December when it
> was snowing. I was in the left lane when another
> truck started sliding. His tractor disappeared and
> then it was all noise and lights. I remember some-
> one coming into my hospital room and saying,
> "We're sorry," and I realized the other truck driver
> was dead.
>
> After that I just couldn't stand to be around
> trucks at all. Every time I'd go close to one I'd
> start to shake. I kept having nightmares and day-
> dreams about the accident. It's not as bad now [2½
> years later] as it was, but they still happen twice a
> week. I don't see faces any more, just outlines.
> After a daydream happens I am more likely to have
> a nightmare, so I try to stay awake as long as I can.
> Wintertimes are worse for me, and I'm still jumpy
> about almost anything like a noise or a fast move-
> ment. I really can't drive much now. I live in a
> small town and go to my folks' farm about three
> miles away on side streets and back roads. If it's
> snowing I don't go at all. If I meet a milk truck on
> the road I pull over and stop and then I start to
> shake and my hands sweat and my heart races.
>
> Someone asked me the other day, "Where is

your pride?'' I don't know where it's gone. I've given up my motorcycles and I haven't bought a hunting license for two years.

I can't face my kids with a clear conscience. I've failed to get back to work, and I can't do things with them, and how do you tell a kid you can't go places like the zoo or shopping? If I do go, by the time I get there I'm no fun to be with. When they ask me why, I say, ''I don't feel good.'' My little girl says, ''But Daddy, you don't look no different.''

Substantial numbers of people who develop acute Post-Traumatic Stress Disorder (acute meaning within six months of the trauma) recover quickly. It seems helpful for those with acute Post-Traumatic Stress Disorder to return as rapidly as possible to full activity and especially to the setting or circumstances in which the trauma occurred. The old saw about ''climbing right back on the horse that threw you'' has real merit. This principle has been employed to good effect by military psychiatrists in the treatment of acute Post-Traumatic Stress Disorder during combat.

For those whose Post-Traumatic Stress Disorder is chronic, which means that it starts or persists beyond six months after the trauma, the course is difficult to predict and impairment may range from mild to very severe and may involve only narrow segments or virtually all aspects of life. While the presence of psychiatric problems before the trauma may increase the likelihood of a Post-Traumatic Stress Disorder, many people who develop Post-Traumatic Stress Disorder have no evidence of previous psychiatric disorder.

Treatment of chronic Post-Traumatic Stress Disorder is less well evolved and less effective than for acute Post-Traumatic Stress Disorder or other Anxiety Disorders. While exposure therapy appears helpful in acute Post-Traumatic Stress Disorder, its role in chronic Post-Traumatic Stress

Disorder is not well-defined. There are case reports of exposure being helpful and other reports that it can heighten rather than reduce anxiety in people suffering from chronic Post-Traumatic Stress Disorder.

One study showed the heightened sensitivity of soldiers suffering Post-Traumatic Stress Disorder to the sights and sounds of battle, even many years later. Three groups of soldiers were studied: 1) a control group who had not experienced combat, 2) a group of combat veterans who had made good post-combat adjustments, and 3) a group of combat veterans whose Post-Traumatic Stress Disorder began at the time of combat and who had poor work and social adjustments upon their return from combat. All three groups heard a tape recording of combat sounds (artillery barrage, bombs falling, and rifle and machine-gun fire) lasting eight minutes and saw flashing lights synchronized with sounds of explosions during the last four minutes of the tape.

The first group (noncombatants) were undisturbed by the experience. On the contrary, after brief increases in attention and heart and breathing rates, they lost interest at times to the point of drowsiness and sleep. All of the members of this first group completed the experiment. The well-adjusted combat veterans showed mild to marked increases in heart and breathing rate and displayed behavioral signs of anxiety: They clasped their hands, startled markedly when light flashes appeared, and described dry mouth, sweating, and feelings of helplessness accompanied by a desire to seek cover or escape. One of 13 subjects in this group stopped the experiment.

The eight combat veterans who had Post-Traumatic Stress Disorder had such severe behavioral reactions that recordings of heart and breathing rates and brain waves were impossible. All subjects appeared very anxious, with some shaking, others crying, three stammering, and one barely able to speak. Five of these eight quit the experiment before the light flashes began. They became severely anxious and restless with thrashing of arms and legs, sweating, and movements to escape. The members of this group had not seen combat for many years.

Persons with chronic Post-Traumatic Stress Disorder may remain very anxious as a result of both internal and external conditioned stimuli. It may be that a narrow range of specific stimuli associated with the trauma has spread, in time, to involve common and innocuous stimuli that are widely present in civilian life.

Antidepressant medications may lift mood and help sleep disturbances, including nightmares, but they seldom reverse the phobic anxiety experienced upon encountering situations that resemble or remind the person of the setting in which the trauma occurred. The value of individual psychotherapeutic and behavioral approaches aimed at reexperiencing the trauma to master it or put it into a realistic past perspective is not clear. Group therapies are being used in Veterans Administration Hospitals and elsewhere with some claims of benefit. Each of the treatments mentioned above has been helpful to some individuals and is worth trying since distress and dysfunction can be quite severe. However, none of these treatments is uniformly effective, and chronic Post-Traumatic Stress Disorder remains a difficult problem whose effective treatment awaits the results of future research.

ADJUSTMENT DISORDER

For a variety of reasons, *adjustment disorders* are in a separate section of *DSM-III*. Nonetheless, one type of adjustment disorder, namely Adjustment Disorder with Anxious Mood, is characterized by anxiety symptoms and is a type of Anxiety Disorder.

An adjustment disorder is an overreaction to a life stress, a response in excess of that normally expected in response to such a stressor (stress-provoking factor). Stressors which could produce adjustment disorders include marital difficulties, business failure, leaving home, and retirement. How a particular person responds to these stressors depends not only on their intensity, but also on the person's vulnerability and other factors such as how much emotional support is available. An adjustment disorder will improve when the stressor is removed or, if this is not possible, when the person learns to live with the continued stressor.

Adjustment disorders, including those with anxiety as the predominant symptom, often improve without treatment. When treatment is necessary, approaches include temporary separation of the person from the stressful situation (this usually does not require hospitalization); ensuring good nutrition, rest, and recreation; occasional short-term use of medication for anxiety and sleep disturbance; and counseling directed at reducing or eliminating the stressor or developing coping strategies for stressors that cannot be removed. The use of behavioral approaches that involve exposure to the stressful situation may be quite beneficial (see Chapter 6). If substantial improvement has not occurred within a few weeks of beginning treatment, careful reevaluation should be done to look for other causes.

SUMMARY

The Anxiety Disorders are the most common psychiatric disorders in the population at large, although smaller numbers of people suffering them receive treatment than those who experience depression or schizophrenia. Most often Anxiety Disorders occur by themselves and if carefully investigated can be distinguished from other disorders of which anxiety is a component. Sometimes Anxiety Disorders come in the wake of depression or medical conditions, and recognition of this sequence is important because treatment of such primary underlying disorders usually relieves the Anxiety Disorder as well.

There has been great interest in diagnosis of different Anxiety Disorders, but no classification system is perfect and further improvements are occurring yearly. For example, debate continues about the frequency with which panic disorder precedes and causes Agoraphobia. The *DSM-III* classification system is an improvement over its predecessor and gives more recognizable descriptions of Anxiety Disorders; this improvement has fostered research on Anxiety Disorders and their treatment.

3

Common Questions About Anxiety and Anxiety Disorders

How common are Anxiety Disorders?

Everyone gets anxious at times. According to a recent survey supported by the National Institute of Mental Health (NIMH), Americans in three large cities (Baltimore, New Haven, and St. Louis) had Anxiety Disorders more frequently than any other mental disorder. The NIMH study surveyed nearly 10,000 people in their homes using the very detailed *Diagnostic Interview Schedule* (DIS). This interview specified the exact wording of questions each person was asked, reducing potential errors due to forgotten questions or changed wording.

Altogether, 8.3 percent of the people who were interviewed had a *DSM-III* Anxiety Disorder (out of a total of 19 percent who had psychiatric disorders). Anxiety Disorders were more common than alcohol and other substance abuse (6.4 percent) or depression and manic depression (6.0 percent).

74

Depression had previously been thought to be the most common disorder, since more patients with depression than anxiety are seen, recognized, and treated by primary care doctors. Some forms of anxiety may be less distressing than depression so that people may not seek treatment; also, doctors may not recognize anxiety as readily as depression, and people may not realize that their anxiety is a disorder which can usually be treated effectively.

Are Anxiety Disorders inherited?

There is a growing body of scientific literature which indicates that individuals with Agoraphobia are more likely than nonagoraphobics to have family members with anxiety and depression. This fits the common finding of depression in patients with diagnosed Anxiety Disorders and vice versa. People with Social Phobia, Blood-Injury Phobia, and—to a lesser degree—Obsessive-Compulsive Disorder, also appear to carry and express a family vulnerability for anxiety and depression. Most blood-injury phobics have a close relative with the same problem.

If two parents have an anxiety or depressive disorder, the chance of a child developing either disorder is greater than if a single parent is troubled. This finding of graded involvement is compatible either with a genetic predisposition to the development of Anxiety Disorders or modeling by relatives (in that same way, being a police officer or a physician tends to run in families).

It is important to realize that many children with one or two parents with anxiety or depressive disorders will not develop either kind of disorder themselves. Although people without a family history of troublesome anxiety or depression are less likely to develop such problems themselves, they may still do so.

The mechanisms by which anxiety is transmitted in families remain unknown. It is now understood why some of those presumed to be vulnerable become symptomatic while other apparently similar individuals remain free of distress. Since several Anxiety Disorders can now be treated effectively, and others may not be severe enough to require treatment, the presence of a family history of Anxiety Disorders should not weigh heavily in decisions people make about marriage partners or having children.

Can parents' attitudes bring on Anxiety Disorders?

Most studies have found that people with Anxiety Disorders come from stable homes with childhood backgrounds similar to those of individuals without Anxiety Disorders. With the exception of Obsessive-Compulsive Disorder, which tends to occur in only children or the oldest child, family size, birth order, parents' ages, deprivation, and amount of psychological disorder in the homes were no different for individuals with Anxiety Disorders compared to people without Anxiety Disorders.

While early observers thought that mothers of agoraphobics were overprotective, careful studies have failed to confirm that impression. Most agoraphobics felt their mothers had been either normally protective or less involved with them than average when they were children. Perhaps doctors' faulty impressions of overprotectiveness came from patients' feelings of resentment that the Anxiety Disorders had caused them to become more dependent on their mothers after the disorder began.

Are children who later developed Anxiety Disorders over-clinging and dependent, fearing separation from their mothers?

School phobia was a bit more common both in phobics and in other disorders such as depression than in people without psychiatric disorders. Histories of other childhood fears—but not of nightmares or behaviors such as bedwetting, thumb sucking, nail biting, truancy, or unusual aggressiveness—were given more frequently by agoraphobics.

The personalities of phobic people are often described as dependent, avoidant, or passive and shy, and both the phobic individuals and those living with them generally agree on these descriptions. Sometimes these characteristics have been present from childhood. Often, they first appear at the time the phobia begins. Obsessive-compulsive individuals may be very insistent or even domineering in requiring others to go along with their rituals. Recognizing that there are obvious exceptions to these generalizations, it seems likely that many of these characterizations are related to behavior that changed because of the Anxiety Disorder rather than preceded it. Thus, an agoraphobic who is fearful of traveling alone may become dependent on others, and a person with Social Phobia who is apprehensive about blushing may be viewed as shy. When an Anxiety Disorder clears up, the affected person's previous personality reemerges. Personalities aren't really changed by Anxiety Disorders.

How can I tell if I have anxiety or panic?

Anxiety has many gradations of intensity. It can be a mere qualm, rise to marked trembling, or become complete panic. Panic is extremely intense anxiety.

The onset and duration of anxiety (or panic) also varies. It may come on gradually over minutes or hours, or it may strike like lightning out of the blue. And it may last for only a few seconds or for hours or even days, although severe panic does not usually last longer than half an hour or so.

Anxiety or panic that bears no relationship to where we are or that has no obvious cause is called *spontaneous anxiety* (or *spontaneous panic*). Anxiety that comes only in particular situations is known as *situational* or *phobic anxiety* (or *phobic panic* if it is severe). Anxiety that is triggered by merely thinking of particular situations is a variety of phobic anxiety (or phobic panic) which is called *anticipatory anxiety* (or *anticipatory panic*).

As far as we can tell, the feelings are similar whether the anxiety (or panic) is spontaneous or phobic. Research has found that the type of phobia also makes little difference to the feelings: Agoraphobics, social phobics, and animal phobics all report similar feelings when in the phobic situation.

Intensity, however, can pull out more stops, depending on the type of anxiety or panic. In experiencing mild tension we might have no more than an unpleasant feeling in the pit of our stomach. The extreme anxiety we call panic brings out a greater orchestration of feelings—we are more likely then to feel rapid heart beat, sweating, and trembling and to think that we are going mad or losing control.

Will an Anxiety Disorder damage my health?

Many people with Anxiety Disorders have suffered from them for decades without apparent injury to their health or development of high blood pressure, ulcers, asthma, or other physical disorders that are commonly thought to result from stress.

A study of medical charts at the University of Iowa found that men and women who had probable diagnoses of Panic Disorder had increased rates of death from suicide, and men had increased rates of death from cardiovascular disease (heart attack, stroke, congestive heart failure), compared to a general population. Another study found no increased death rate in patients with Panic Disorder.

It is our strong impression that Anxiety Disorders on the whole shorten people's lives little, if at all, and they certainly shorten life far less than do common bad habits such as smoking, intemperate drinking, and overconsumption of fatty foods. Whether Panic Disorder shortens people's lives needs more study.

Why do I feel like fainting—but never actually faint— during a panic?

Fear of fainting or collapsing is common during panic. Dizziness or feeling faint occurred in 83 percent of panic patients surveyed in one study.

Feeling faint stems from *hypertension* or overbreathing. Some people who feel faint while anxious are unaware that they are hyperventilating. Close observation, however, often reveals that they are overbreathing.

Anxiety and fear cause faster breathing both in people with and without Anxiety Disorders. Hyperventilation often begins as a reaction to a feeling that the person cannot catch his or her breath. The changes caused by hyperventilation further frighten the person, and a vicious cycle of overbreathing and greater fear ensues. Nearly all of the symptoms associated with panic can be caused by hyperventilation.

Although hyperventilation causes a feeling of faintness and some claim actual fainting as well, we have never seen a person faint while hyperventilating. In contrast, most blood-injury phobics have fainted repeatedly at the sight of blood or injury. Rarely, hyperventilating people feel so faint that they lie down, shut their eyes, and stop talking, but they still remain aware of what is happening to and around them rather than passing out altogether.

Learning to control hyperventilation helps some people with anxiety. (See below for a description of a hyperventilation test and techniques to control hyperventilation.)

What exactly is hyperventilation?

Hyper (too much) *ventilation* (air movement) is "overbreathing"

—that is, breathing that is more than is needed to meet the body's demands of oxygen and removal of carbon dioxide. Many hyperventilation symptoms are physical reactions that occur rapidly as a result of changes in levels of certain components of the blood called *electrolytes,* such as carbon dioxide, bicarbonate, calcium, and phosphorus. Forceful hyperventilation can reduce the carbon dioxide level in the blood by 50 percent in as little as 30 seconds. Although we learned in school that carbon dioxide is a waste product of the body's metabolism that must be gotten rid of, we actually need *some* carbon dioxide to feel and function well. Hyperventilation lowers carbon dioxide levels too much below their normal level and produces distressing symptoms.

Hyperventilation can occur when breathing is rapid or deep or both. Even sighing can be a form of hyperventilation, while others experience dramatic changes in the way they feel and function. All of the symptoms associated with panic can be brought on by hyperventilation, including shortness of breath (*dyspnea*); rapid or irregular heart beat (*palpitations*); chest pain or discomfort; choking or smothering sensations; dizziness, vertigo, or unsteady feelings; feelings of unreality; tingling in the hands, feet, or lips (*paresthesias*); hot and cold flashes; sweating; faintness; and trembling or shaking. A few people with Panic Disorder report that hyperventilation brings on actual panics. Most people with Panic Disorder report that hyperventilation produces some, but not all, of their panic symptoms.

How can I tell if hyperventilation is a problem for me?

Counting your breathing rate (or having someone else do it at a time when you are not aware that it is being counted) is a good starting point. Normal breathing rates at rest range from as low as eight to as high as 16 times per minute. Some people with hyperventilation find that their breathing rate is above this limit, and one study of patients with Panic Disorder found an average resting breathing rate of 28 per minute.

Since it is possible to hyperventilate by breathing very deeply at a normal rate, a hyperventilation test may be helpful. While there is no standard hyperventilation test, the principle is to breath rapidly and deeply for a few minutes to see what effects hyperventilation will have. One specific test asks people to breathe 60 times a minute (once every second) for three minutes. Everyone who attempts this test will notice feelings of dry mouth and throat, and many people report some lightheadedness, slight changes in vision, and numbness and tingling. However, when this test was used with a group of patients suffering from Panic Disorder, 67 percent could not continue for two minutes because of symptoms they experienced. In a group of individuals without Panic Disorder, only 4 percent would not continue the test for the full three minutes.

Although the hyperventilation test is not conclusive concerning the role of hyperventilation in producing symptoms associated with panic, it may be quite helpful in making a distinction. There are some medical conditions such as angina (heart pain) and seizures (epilepsy) that can be made worse by hyperventilation. If in doubt about whether this test is safe for you, consult your doctor.

What can be done to control hyperventilation?
Several things can be done to control hyperventilation, each of which may be helpful for different individuals.

A hyperventilation test (described above) may be helpful in establishing the role of hyperventilation in producing some of the symptoms associated with panic. If overbreathing provokes anxiety, then control of hyperventilation may prevent or relieve those symptoms. Knowing that hyperventilation symptoms can be very distressing but are not harmful provides some comfort even while these symptoms are occurring.

Specific techniques to gain control of overbreathing are also available:

1. Cover your mouth and nose with a small paper bag and breathe into and out of it. This technique causes some rebreathing of the carbon dioxide that you have just exhaled.
2. Slow your breathing rate by using a clock to breathe (for example, breathe just once every five seconds, or 12 times a minute). This technique can bring runaway breathing under control.
3. Consciously take smaller breaths; this will reduce the volume of air being moved with each breath.
4. Try *belly breathing* (breathing mainly with the diaphragm and not with the chest) to control hyperventilation. One technique for learning belly breathing is to spread your hands and fingers around your ribcage and then breathe, as much as possible, by merely moving your belly in and out and keeping your ribcage nearly still. As your belly moves in and out, it reflects the movements of the diaphragm, which provides ample ventilation for a person at rest.
5. Rehearse the words ''slow and shallow'' to the point at which they become a reflex thought when symptoms of hyperventilation appear.

All of these methods decrease overbreathing and help to restore the blood electrolytes (carbon dioxide, bicarbonate, calcium, and phosphorus) to normal levels. As the ventilation of the lungs and the blood's electrolytes return to normal, the symptoms of hyperventilation disappear.

Practicing methods to control overbreathing provides many who suffer panics with something useful to do when panic occurs. There is some evidence that combining these methods with exposure therapy improves results in people who hyperventilate as part of their panic or other Anxiety Disorder. However, it does not appear that methods to control overbreathing are sufficient by themselves to overcome Anxiety Disorders. Exposure therapy—and, in some patients, medications—are usually necessary.

Is it normal to have anxiety and fear?

It's abnormal *not* to have anxiety and fear in response to certain situations. As one joke goes, "Anyone who remains calm under *these* circumstances just doesn't understand what's happening." Anxiety that doesn't overwhelm us can help us do some things better. Knowing that we have to give a talk in a class or act before an audience evokes anxiety that often leads us to careful preparation, practice, and rehearsal, all of which is likely to improve our performance. Slight fear can mobilize us to "fight or flight" and is protective, increasing our chances of survival. There is a limit to this process, however. When fear becomes overwhelming it can paralyze people and prevent them from acting normally in the face of danger. Most people can learn to function well even in the face of fear and danger, and we recognize courage and bravery as laudable human values.

Anxiety and fear can be helpful or harmful. The circumstances in which they occur, their duration, and their severity all combine to determine the net benefit or cost of anxiety and fear. As with most things, there is no absolute good or bad in anxiety and fear: The context in which they occur and the extent to which they improve or impair functioning determine whether they are normal and helpful or abnormal and destructive.

What are the chances that a person will act out frightening obsessions?

Many people with Obsessive-Compulsive Disorder suffer from a horrifying idea, urge, or impulse to hurt someone, often a family member or close friend. At times they worry they may have struck someone with their car. This obsession leads them to retrace their path in anguished searching for evidence of their "hit and run" accident or to look for accounts of their presumed "crime" in the next day's newspapers. Some are afraid to describe their obsessions for fear they will be reported to the police or committed to a mental hospital. Some experience an urge to blurt out confessions to crimes they haven't committed and may take elaborate precautions to tape-record their telephone conversations or make copies of any written materials they send out (including checks or even paper money) in attempts to reassure themselves that they have neither committed nor confessed any crime.

It is easy to understand how distressing these obsessions are and, if revealed to others, how alarming they might seem. Usually, however, the obsessions expressed are so patently ridiculous that a person who hears them discounts them immediately and attempts to reassure the person that the fears are unfounded. This reassurance may help for a brief period, but the obsessions return and the cycle is likely to be repeated many times.

The chance is very small that people with obsessions involving injuring others will act out their obsessions. We know of only two out of 400 cases in which people with obsessions acted on their urges, and one of these two persons had previously been assaultive and was psychotic (had lost contact with reality) at the time of the assault.

Sometimes schizophrenia is mistaken for Obsessive-

Compulsive Disorder. Rarely, people with schizophrenia hear voices commanding them to do dangerous things, and it is even more rare for them to carry out these instructions. The distinction between Obsessive-Compulsive Disorder and schizophrenia is usually straightforward, and for an individual with Obsessive-Compulsive Disorder to act out harmful obsessive fears is exceedingly rare.

Are Anxiety Disorders caused by a chemical imbalance?
All thoughts and feelings—including anxiety—result from complex electrochemical reactions in the nervous system. However, the fact that antidepressant and antianxiety drugs can reduce certain kinds of anxiety tells us little about which chemical reactions are involved; these treatments may only bring about secondary electrochemical reactions that are actually remote from the original source of the chemical imbalance. The important point is this: Whatever the causes of anxiety, sufferers can be helped and can learn to help themselves.

Behavioral treatments have also been shown to be very effective in treating several Anxiety Disorders, sometimes without the use of any medication. Because of this, some doctors believe that the ways that people think can contribute to or relieve their anxiety. Certain surroundings and activities are more frightening than others, although this is a highly individual matter and one person's "passion" may be another's "poison."

So while some Anxiety Disorders may be caused by chemical imbalances, others may be due to psychosocial factors. The causes of anxiety give no clear guide to treatment, however, and various methods—behavior, medical, psychodynamic, and even (very rarely) surgical—have a part to play in relieving anxiety.

What role does stress play in causing anxiety and Anxiety Disorders?

Although stress causes anxiety, there is little evidence that it causes Anxiety Disorders, with the exception of Post-Traumatic Stress Disorder and Adjustment Disorder with Anxious Mood. Stressors (stress-provoking factors) such as speaking in public or working under a tight deadline often make people anxious. If the anxiety is not extreme, it usually helps mobilize the person to prepare and perform well. If anxiety rises too high, however, people may become unable to deal with the situation they are in or to act normally. Different people vary in their capacities to tolerate and benefit from anxiety, and each person's ability to cope with anxiety and danger varies somewhat from time to time.

With the exceptions of Post-Traumatic Stress Disorder, which follows extreme stress beyond a person's tolerance, and Adjustment Disorder with Anxious Mood, which is an overreaction to a psychosocial stressor, it is not clear that stress is important in causing Anxiety Disorders. Even where the stress seems causative, it is often impossible to specify exactly how this operates. The role that stress plays in causing Anxiety Disorders is undefined at present.

How can I fight an Anxiety Disorder?

A trite answer is to do the things that decrease anxiety and avoid the things that increase it. While it seems to make sense to avoid something that brings on anxiety caused by an Anxiety Disorder (and some well-meaning friends and even doctors may say, "If it bothers you, just stay away from it"), avoiding the things that make us anxious usually makes the Anxiety Disorders worse. Two studies have shown that phobics who avoid the things they fear may get worse, yet the same people improve if they face the things they fear. The same is true for people with Obsessive-Compulsive Disorder.

There may be three exceptions to the rule that facing fear makes it better. First, about 3 percent of people with Anxiety Disorders do not improve when they expose themselves to the things they fear. The reasons why this very small proportion of patients fail to respond to exposure are not known at this time.

Second, some individuals suffering from chronic Post-Traumatic Stress Disorder may find that exposure to the scene of their trauma—or even exposure to similar scenes in television shows, movies, magazines, or newspapers—will recreate feelings of great anxiety. This is very unlike the experience of people with Phobic and Obsessive-Compulsive Disorders who are pleasantly surprised that their anxiety actually decreases when they face the thing they fear.

Third, anxiety about a real danger (such as being the victim of a mugging in a neighborhood in which such attacks are common) should not be treated by exposure. This is an example of anxiety that aids survival. Exposure to this situation would increase the risk of actual harm and is obviously not appropriate.

It is not known why exposure is so successful for the large majority of patients with Anxiety Disorders yet apparently ineffective for a small minority (about 3 percent of persons with Phobic or Obsessive-Compulsive Disorders and a larger proportion of persons who suffer from chronic Post-Traumatic Stress Disorder).

Therefore, most people with phobias and obsessive-compulsive rituals can "fight" them by facing the things they fear and by remaining in contact with them until their anxiety lessens and becomes manageable. Repeated exposure sessions are very effective treatment for these people.

(We don't yet have conclusive evidence about the effectiveness of exposure as treatment for people with Panic Disorder without Agoraphobia, Generalized Anxiety Disorder, and Post-Traumatic Stress Disorder.)

Can hypoglycemia cause anxiety?

Hypoglycemia (low blood sugar) can cause a variety of emotional and physical symptoms. These include anxiety as well as headache, lightheadedness, palpitations, sweating, shakiness, weakness, hunger, fatigue, nausea, and vomiting. It is important to realize that most people with anxiety do not have hypoglycemia, despite the overtendency of some health care "professionals" to blame many physical and emotional problems on low blood sugar. The unfortunate tendency to overdiagnose hypoglycemia may in fact hide the correct diagnosis and lead to inappropriate treatment. The diagnosis of hypoglycemia can be made conclusively only by actually finding abnormally low levels of sugar in several blood samples when symptoms are present. Clear relief of symptoms when blood sugar is raised to normal helps to confirm the diagnosis. In the rare instances in which anxiety is due to hypoglycemia, there are specific, effective medical treatments that are available to correct hypoglycemia.

Can allergies cause anxiety?

This is a controversial issue. Recent studies have shown that hypersensitivity to certain foods can cause psychological symptoms in some people. However, the most carefully done research suggests that this is quite uncommon. Nonetheless, a movement known as Clinical Ecology holds that many illnesses, including those with anxiety, are frequently caused by hypersensitivity or "allergic" reactions to a wide variety of environmental substances; the mainstream of medicine regards these claims as extravagant and unsubstantiated and feels that very few people have anxiety symptoms that could be attributed to allergies. More extensive and well-designed research studies are needed to help resolve this controversy.

Can a hormone imbalance cause anxiety?

Yes, a hormone imbalance can cause anxiety, but this anxiety is usually part of a group of symptoms which would suggest to your physician that a particular hormonal disorder is present. It would be quite rare for anxiety to be the only symptom in the case of a hormone imbalance. Also, anxiety and a hormonal disorder may coexist yet be unrelated.

Hormonal or endocrine disorders that may cause anxiety include thyroid gland overactivity (*hyperthyroidism* or *thyrotoxicosis*) or underactivity (*hypothyroidism* or *myxedema*), adrenal gland overactivity (*hyperadrenalism* or *Cushing's syndrome*), parathyroid gland overactivity (*hyperparathyroidism*) or underactivity (*hypoparathyroidism*), and the premenstrual syndrome (see below). Hormonal drugs like steroids (cortisone, prednisone, and others) occasionally have anxiety-like side effects.

When anxiety is caused by a hormonal disturbance, correction of the underlying problem should relieve the symptoms. A comprehensive evaluation of anxiety should include attention to the endocrine system.

Can anxiety be part of the premenstrual syndrome?

Yes, anxiety is one of many symptoms that have been ascribed to the premenstrual syndrome (PMS). Other emotional symptoms may include irritability, impatience, restlessness, tension, fatigue, sadness, and depression. By definition, symptoms associated with PMS are either confined to or greatly aggravated during the premenstrual part of the cycle. Keeping a daily record of symptoms over several cycles can be quite useful to the patient's doctor in making a diagnosis. At present there are many treatments available for PMS, but none has been shown to be uniformly effective.

What about the "nuclear phobia" that has recently been mentioned in the news?

Use of the term "nuclear phobia" has led many people to wonder whether their concerns about a nuclear holocaust are irrational. A phobia, by definition, involves an irrational fear, one that is out of proportion with the risks the individual actually faces. Thus, a fear of flying that leads someone to drive across country can be labeled a phobia, because the risks of driving are actually many times greater than those of flying. If a person withdrew from life, built a bomb shelter, and never left it, that behavior would be irrational, and a label of nuclear phobia would then be appropriate. Concerns about a nuclear war causing death for the individual—and possibly, the human race—are not irrational. These concerns make good sense, they are shared by very many people who are entirely rational, and they may eventually lead to a more constructive approach to control of nuclear weapons.

We feel the use of the term phobia is incorrect for the concern that many people experience regarding the risk of injury or death from an accidental or planned nuclear incident.

4

Do I Have Anxiety
Needing Treatment?

EVERYONE has had unpleasant and distressing experiences which lead to anxiety. This anxiety is short-lived and goes away when the unpleasant experiences stop or when ways are found to deal with the problem, often stimulated in part by the presence of anxiety. The boundary between normal anxiety and anxiety that requires treatment is not sharply defined. Some people seek treatment for anxiety that disappears spontaneously in a few days. Some doctors don't start treatment until they are absolutely certain that a clear Anxiety Disorder is present and is interfering with the individual's functioning. These different boundary lines for deciding when to seek and to offer treatment are understandable, considering the state of our current knowledge about anxiety, the different attitudes of various individuals about seeking and offering help, and the availability of effective treatments.

Most doctors agree that Anxiety Disorders should be treated if they hamper social functioning, intimate relationships, education, or work adjustment. Many also agree that treatment should be considered when a person is suffering from distressing anxiety, even though the individual is able to function in most life situations. In the end, decisions regarding the need for treatment are best made on individual grounds by the patient, the patient's family, and the doctor involved.

Given that some disagreements remain about the diagnosis of Anxiety Disorders, what help is available for identifying anxiety that might need treatment? A number of paper-and-pencil questionnaires have been developed to help with screening for Phobic and Obsessive-Compulsive Disorders. People who have concerns about their own situation can use these to help in the decision of whether to seek treatment.

The Fear Questionnaire (page 94) and the Obsessive-Compulsive Checklist (pages 95–96) can help in determining whether a person actually has an Anxiety Disorder. They have been used to help indicate the severity of such disorders and to measure the change in anxiety over the course of treatment. Both questionnaires have appeared previously in the book *Living With Fear* (Copyright © 1978 McGraw-Hill; reproduced with permission).

FEAR QUESTIONNAIRE

The Fear Questionnaire provides an opportunity for a person to rank his or her reactions to 15 specific situations that might provoke anxiety, plus any other situations that the person wishes to add. In addition, the Fear Questionnaire includes room for the individual to define in his or her own words the main phobia they want to have treated. The ranking is done on a scale from 0 (Would not avoid it) to 8 (Always avoid it).

The Fear Questionnaire is scored by adding the scores for items 1 to 5 to obtain a subtotal for Agoraphobia, adding the scores for items 6 to 10 to obtain a subtotal for Blood-Injury Phobia, and adding the scores for items 11 through 15 to obtain a subtotal for Social Phobia. A score for any of the three separate five-item clusters (Agoraphobia, Blood-Injury Phobia, Social Phobia) from 10 to 17 suggests a mild phobic problem, and a score from 18 upwards strongly suggests that a phobic disorder may be present.

It is important not to depend too heavily on measures such as the Fear Questionnaire for guidance. Although it is useful in measuring change in response to treatment, and permits comparisons with a large population of people with Anxiety Disorders, some people with severe phobias could have normal scores on the Fear Questionnaire merely because the questionnaire does not cover their phobia or because they minimize their distress. Simple phobias, for example, are not assessed by the questionnaire.

OBSESSIVE-COMPULSIVE CHECKLIST

Obsessions and compulsions may be partly described by the extent to which an individual tends to avoid certain situations, is slow in completing them, or repeats them. The Obsessive-Compulsive Checklist permits an individual to rate these aspects of functioning for activities that are commonly difficult for obsessive-compulsives. In general, total scores above 10 raise a question about Obsessive-Compulsive Disorder, while those above 20 indicate it even more strongly.

FEAR QUESTIONNAIRE

Choose a number from the scale below to show how much you
avoid each of the situations listed, because of fear or other unpleasant feelings. Then write the number you chose in the box
opposite each situation.

0	1	2	3	4	5	6	7	8

Would not avoid it	*Slightly avoid it*	*Definitely avoid it*	*Markedly avoid it*	*Always avoid it*

1. Traveling alone by bus or plane
2. Walking alone in busy streets
3. Going into crowded stores
4. Going alone far from home
5. Large open spaces
6. Injections or minor surgery
7. Hospitals
8. Sight of blood
9. Thought of injury or illness
10. Going to the dentist
11. Eating or drinking with other people
12. Being watched or stared at
13. Talking to people in authority
14. Being criticized
15. Speaking or acting to an audience
16. Other situations (describe, e.g., animals, thunder)

Total ☐

Below describe in your own words the *main* phobia you want
treated (e.g., "shopping alone in a busy supermarket" or "fluttering
birds"):

Rate how bad it is in this box.   ☐

It is important to keep in mind that the Obsessive-Compulsive Checklist is only an indicator of the *possibility* of Obsessive-Compulsive Disorder. Even if an individual shows clear obsessive-compulsive behaviors, careful evaluation and diagnosis is necessary to discriminate among the many possible causes of such behavior. A few obsessive-compulsive behaviors that may be severely disabling are not represented in the checklist, and some obsessive-compulsive people do not actively report their distress or they tend to minimize its effect.

OBSESSIVE-COMPULSIVE CHECKLIST

People with your kind of problem occasionally have difficulty with some of the following activities. Answer each question by writing the appropriate number in the box next to it.

0   *No problem with activity—takes me same time as average person. I do not need to repeat or avoid it.*

1   *Activity takes me twice as long as most people, or I have to repeat it twice, or I tend to avoid it.*

2   *Activity takes me three times as long as most people, or I have to repeat it three or more times, or I usually avoid it.*

Score	Activity	Score	Activity
	Taking a bath or shower		Touching own genitals, petting, or sexual intercourse
	Washing hands and face		
	Care of hair (e.g., washing, combing, brushing)		Throwing things away
			Visiting a hospital
	Brushing teeth		Turning lights and taps on or off
	Dressing and undressing		
	Using toilet to urinate		Locking or closing doors or windows
	Using toilet to defecate		

Score	Activity	Score	Activity
	Touching people or being touched		Using electrical appliance (e.g., heaters)
	Handling waste or waste bins		Doing arithmetic or accounts
	Washing clothing		Getting to work
	Washing dishes		Doing own work
	Handling or cooking food		Writing
	Cleaning the house		Form filling
	Keeping things tidy		Mailing letters
	Bed making		Reading
	Cleaning shoes		
	Touching door handles		Total

DIAGNOSIS

The Fear Questionnaire and the Obsessive-Compulsive Check-list cannot be used to replace a doctor's diagnosis of Anxiety Disorder, but they are helpful screening devices. In the United States, Anxiety Disorders are diagnosed on the basis of *DSM-III*, and in other countries the *International Classification of Diseases* is used. Please refer to pages 19–20 for a discussion of the purposes of diagnosis. *DSM-III* is designed for use by doctors and was not written for use by patients; therefore, some people will find the terminology of *DSM-III* difficult to understand. Because many will find *DSM-III* informative, Appendix A contains the chapter from *DSM-III* that deals with Anxiety Disorders.

Anxiety is also a component of some other *DSM-III* disorders (such as Adjustment Disorder with Anxious Mood), and anxiety is often seen in other psychiatric disorders such as delirium, drug withdrawal reactions, schizophrenia, depression, hypochondriasis, and sexual dysfunction. Each of these disorders has specific criteria for diagnosis, but these are not included in this book.

Diagnosis requires careful consideration of many factors, including the individual's medical and psychiatric histories, family history, response to treatment, and present symptoms (what patients complain of) and signs (what doctors observe). An open mind, strong powers of observation, continuing study of diagnostic advances, patience, and experience combine to make a doctor an excellent diagnostician. If the diagnosis is not clear or if the response to treatment is less than satisfactory, both patient and doctor may benefit from a consultation or second opinion.

Many people with typical Phobic and Obsessive-Compulsive Disorders will be able to recognize their own situations in the descriptions provided in this book; for them, evaluation and diagnosis by an experienced doctor is most necessary to make sure that there is not some medical problem causing or aggravating the Anxiety Disorder. We hope that you will take any concerns or questions that arise from your reading to your doctor, so that you are most likely to receive expert evaluation and treatment.

LABORATORY TESTS

Several new laboratory tests that have been developed to identify Anxiety Disorders are currently being evaluated. So far, none of these tests remotely approaches the diagnostic value of a few simple questions about what is feared and avoided. These tests attempt to identify markers of abnormalities in biological function that suggest a likelihood of

Anxiety Disorder. Examples of such tests include a search for abnormalities of common and accessible physiological functioning such as heart and breathing rate, size of the pupil of the eye, muscle tension, and amount of sweating in individuals who are exposed to the things they fear. Some of these measurements must be made under closely controlled conditions (of sound and temperature) in a laboratory, and others are difficult to interpret because of differences in what is considered "normal" for different individuals. In general, the reliability of these physiologic measurements outside closely controlled laboratory conditions is too low to be of value in the routine care of patients, and they are presently useful only in research settings to help answer specific research questions.

Another line of laboratory tests seeks to provoke symptoms of panic in susceptible individuals by an intravenous infusion of a substance such as sodium lactate or isoproterenol. The researchers who developed this test theorize that a positive reaction would confirm the presence of Panic Disorder and possibly rule out other causes for the anxiety. The most consistent results so far have been obtained with sodium lactate infusions, but even then no more than one-half of the subjects with clear-cut, diagnosed Panic Disorders develop panic during the test if they and their doctors are not told when they are receiving the sodium lactate infusion.

Measurement of changes in blood levels of brain and body neurotransmitters and their breakdown products (*metabolites*)—as well as measurement of levels of fatty acids or other blood components that indirectly indicate levels of neurotransmitters and hormones—are all being investigated with an eye to developing more objective laboratory tests for anxiety.

More routine laboratory tests, such as blood counts and blood chemistries, hormone levels, electrocardiograms and electroencephalograms, and x-rays and other body imaging techniques, might all be useful to evaluate and exclude the presence of medical disorders that may be causing anxiety.

The search for accurate and reliable laboratory tests that will be useful in identifying Anxiety Disorders continues, but no tests have been discovered and refined to the point that they can be recommended at this time. Until such laboratory tests are evaluated, clarified, and standardized, conscientious physicians will continue to rely on other means (see Summary below) to successfully evaluate patients with Anxiety Disorders.

SUMMARY

While some Anxiety Disorders are easily diagnosed, a comprehensive diagnosis of Anxiety Disorder rests on a careful history of present symptoms and past episodes, family history, observations of the patient, and reports of family members. Consideration of all of these factors yields the best diagnosis and decision about the need for treatment. At times, the diagnosis may be unclear and a further period of careful observation may prove helpful. At other times when the diagnosis is unclear, the patient and doctor may decide to begin treatment because distress is of such magnitude that waiting is unjustified.

With the development and refinement of diagnostic tools such as the Fear Questionnaire and the Obsessive-Compulsive Checklist and of diagnostic systems like *DSM-III*—and with further strides in the fields of epidemiology (the study of the frequency and the distribution of disorders or illness), basic science, and laboratory research—both diagnosis and treatment of Anxiety Disorders will become more refined and successful.

5

How Is Anxiety Treated?

JUST as there are different factors that may cause different Anxiety Disorders, so there are different treatments for them. Sometimes these therapies are aimed directly at the presumed causes of the anxiety disorder. More often, these therapies are given because they have been shown to be generally helpful or because the doctor is most familiar with their use.

One of the first rules of medicine is *"Primum non nocere,"* meaning, "First, do no harm." The history of medicine is littered with examples of well-intentioned treatments that hurt more than they helped. Richard Asher, a practical and clear-thinking English physician, wrote, "It is important to realize that ideas are much easier to believe if they are comforting, and that many clinical notions are accepted because they are comforting rather than because there is any evidence to support them." An earlier English physician, Sir Clifford Albutt, might have been writing about today's medicine rather than that of the 1890s: "Our path is cumbered with guesses, presumptions, and conjectures, the untimely and sterile fruitage of minds which cannot bear to wait for the facts, and are ready to forget that the use of hypotheses lies, not in the display of ingenuity, but in the labor of verification." These wise physicians remind us that much of medical therapeutics is based on belief and that scientific proof of effectiveness is difficult to obtain.

Common sense suggests that when anxiety arises, we should review our everyday habits to see whether we have neglected the foundation on which we build our functioning. William Osler, the most famous physician at the start of the Twentieth Century, felt that "patients should have good food, fresh air, rest, and exercise—the quadrangle of health." He wrote this at a time when less could be done for serious diseases, but his excellent advice remains valid for the three-quarters or more of self-remitting ills from which humans suffer.

Since anxiety is a normal and often helpful human state, total freedom from anxiety would be a misguided goal. If anxiety signals uncertainty in the face of an unfamiliar challenge, then preparation and rehearsal are needed and the anxiety is therefore helpful. Even anxiety associated with life-threatening challenges ranging from operating a motor vehicle to combat can be channeled into risk-reducing behaviors by careful planning and repeated practice.

When anxiety reaches levels where it interferes with rather than stimulates functioning, evaluation and treatment are needed. Treatment should not be prescribed without a thorough evaluation, because the types of anxiety range from those that respond to simple measures through those requiring sophisticated behavioral, drug, or psychotherapeutic treatment. Some individuals may need medical treatments of primary medical problems instead of or in addition to treatment of an Anxiety Disorder, and a very few patients may even need psychosurgery, although this is very rare. Inevitably, there are a few cases of Anxiety Disorder for which known treatments are ineffective.

Treatments should be selected on the basis of their scientifically demonstrated effectiveness, efficiency of administration, cost, patient preference, and availability of capable therapists.

Behavior therapies form the cornerstone for the treatment of Phobic and Obsessive-Compulsive Disorders. In those conditions the effectiveness of behavior therapies has been conclusively proven through scientific research. Many sufferers can treat themselves with these methods, by using the techniques described in Chapter 11. Those who cannot manage this self-treatment could seek help from a behavior therapist. Pages 106–111 describe behavior therapy in more detail.

Medications also play an important role in the treatment of Anxiety Disorders, sometimes complementing behavior therapies. The effectiveness of antidepressant and antianxiety medications has been shown for certain patients with Anxiety Disorders, but the effects may wear off when the medication is stopped and side effects can be troublesome. Antianxiety drugs are commonly used both safely and effectively on a short-term basis to treat troublesome situational anxiety, such as that associated with serious injury or illness. The use of medications is described more fully in Chapter 7.

Supportive relationships have been shown to form a very effective component in the treatment of Anxiety Disorders. Every patient should have the benefit of support and empathic understanding during the course of treatment of an

Anxiety Disorder, but this support need not come from a professional. Friends and relatives can often serve in these supportive roles quite well.

Doctors should provide explanations of the particular Anxiety Disorder and its treatment (with the patient's permission) to family members, friends, and others who are important in the patient's life (in fact, we hope that this book can be one of the tools used to help explain Anxiety Disorders in such situations). These individuals constitute a valuable network of support that is more readily available than any other support method that a doctor can provide. When other treatments are ineffective, support by others who care can sustain a person until anxiety may resolve on its own with the passage of time.

Dynamic and *analytic psychotherapies* have a more ambitious goal: to effectively alleviate symptoms of the Anxiety Disorder by uncovering psychological causes of the Anxiety Disorder and by helping patients to attain insights about themselves and to bring about changes in their personality characteristics and behaviors that may prevent recurrence of the Anxiety Disorder. Many doctors believe that underlying psychological conflicts are responsible for some Anxiety Disorders and that psychotherapy directed at identifying and resolving these conflicts is the best treatment for these individuals. However, there is little scientific evidence supporting the effectiveness of dynamic and analytic psychotherapy for Anxiety Disorders. In fairness to these treatment approaches, we would also like to point out that dynamic and analytic psychotherapy have not been conclusively shown to be ineffective. See Chapter 8 for further information on psychotherapy of Anxiety Disorders.

Other treatments such as exercise and psychosurgery are controversial and are the subject of ongoing research. Both of these treatments appear to be useful for a small group of patients. See Chapter 9 for more information.

The treatments mentioned above have varying roles in the treatment of Anxiety Disorders. Whatever treatment is used, it is important for each patient to understand the reasons that particular treatment was selected, what to expect in terms of improvements and side effects, and what to do if treatment does not proceed as expected. Selecting the best treatment for each patient requires knowledge, experience, skills, and—frankly—sometimes luck. When one treatment is ineffective, another may yet be successful. Optimism that a successful treatment will be found, persistence in pursuit of a successful treatment, and flexibility in matching a patient with the best treatment are hallmarks of good therapy. Each class of treatments will be discussed in more detail in the following chapters.

6

Behavior Therapy

I N the last 20 years the behavioral approach to therapy
has revolutionized the treatment of persistent phobias
and obsessive-compulsive rituals. This approach is based
on old principles, but these are applied with a new thoroughness
that can bring reliable relief of suffering that previously
might have continued unchanged for decades. Behavior
therapy does not assume that phobias and rituals are sym-
bolic transformations of hidden difficulties. Instead, it regards the phobia or ritual itself as the main handicap and
tries to eliminate this handicap directly—not by uncovering
unconscious meanings, but by teaching the sufferer how to
face those situations that trigger discomfort and how to
eventually come to tolerate them. For some people, problems that have been present for 30 years or more have been
overcome in a few hours of exposure over a couple of days.

Effective treatment usually takes somewhat longer, though—perhaps several weeks or months.

Not all behavioral methods are equally effective. Relaxation is often called a behavior therapy, but it does not reduce phobias or rituals. The many variants of behavioral approaches that are effective have in common the principle of *exposure to that which frightens you until you get used to it*. Once you confront your fear with determination, it will diminish. We don't know quite how or why this method works. But it does work, provided that exposure continues long enough.

In fact you can observe the process at work even with very simple animals. If you touch the antennae of a snail, they will quickly retract; after a minute or two the snail will put out its antennae once more. Touch them again and they will be drawn back a second time, but on this occasion a bit less quickly, and after a shorter interval they will creep out again. Touch them a third time, and a fourth time, and a fifth, and progressively the snail will get used to your touch and its antennae will eventually stop retreating from your finger. Through repeated exposure to this provoking activity, the snail's "anxiety" has been extinguished. This simple process, called *habituation*, is similar to the way that phobics and ritualizers react during exposure therapy. Habituation has been shown to last for weeks in snails and for many years in humans. In other words, improvement in phobic and ritualizing behaviors can endure, provided that the habituation by exposure has been sufficiently thorough.

COMMON QUESTIONS ABOUT BEHAVIOR THERAPY

How long should exposure sessions last?
There is no quick answer beyond "longer is better." In a

lucky minority of sufferers, just a few minutes of exposure
to the things that terrify them can lead to a reduction in fear.
This might be especially true for those who have not had
their phobias for long and who are really determined to get
the better of them. More commonly the fear starts to
diminish within half an hour after the start of the exposure,
even in people with very long-standing phobias or rituals.
Rarely, several hours of exposure over time may be needed
for the discomfort to start abating. The important point is to
persevere until the anxiety starts to lessen and to be prepared to go on until it does.

How rapidly should I tackle my worst fears?

It is understandable that many people with Anxiety Disorders want to undertake therapy little by little, proceeding
slowly from their easiest to their worst fears. In general,
however, the more rapidly you tackle your worst fears the
more quickly you will recover. The faster and longer we
embrace the monster panic during exposure therapy, the
more rapidly it will fade in our arms to become a mere
shadow of itself, recognizable as mild tension rather than
terror.

Can anxiety during exposure be harmful?

Contrary to popular belief, the answer is usually no. In the
past, physicians and psychologists were reluctant to allow
patients to become very frightened because they thought that
serious harm could result. Now we know that the great
majority of people who are given the chance to experience
extreme panic eventually become unable to experience more
than mild fear. Paradoxically, if we try to panic, the odds
are that we won't be able to, or that we will produce only a
pale reflection of the real thing. Even if severe panic does
strike, it will gradually evaporate and become less likely to

return in the future. In a curious way, really effective exposure treatments for anxiety could develop only as therapists learned to endure the anxiety of their patients, secure in the knowledge that it is unlikely to harm but instead that it will lead to their improvement.

Can I use exposure therapy by myself?

Yes, if you are prepared to go about it with a will and be really systematic. Over the last few years we have learned that phobics who, by themselves, followed the self-help instructions in Chapter 10 can achieve great and lasting improvement—in fact, as much improvement as when they follow the same instructions from a psychiatrist. And we have more recently discovered that some obsessive-compulsives, too, can overcome their rituals on their own by applying the same principles. Those who find it a bit intimidating to follow these procedures without professional help could start off with that help and then gradually shoulder the responsibility themselves.

Remember that the professional's task is essentially to coach you in the exposure principle and to monitor your progress. With exposure therapy, *you* are your own therapist, even when therapy is initiated and supervised by your doctor. While the doctor advises and encourages you, it is you who carries out the homework assignments required to make really worthwhile gains. And given a proper framework, most people are able to treat themselves with relatively little time required of the professional. This is an important discovery of recent years.

Will exposure help prevent phobias from developing after I've been frightened?

There is a golden rule for nipping phobias and rituals in the bud: *Avoid escape!* Encourage yourself to face your fears.

For example, after a sudden accident with a car, a bicycle, or a horse, the vital thing to do is to resume driving or riding *immediately* so that you won't brood about the situation and the anxiety that it provoked. Going right back to face the feared situation will prevent you from becoming sensitized to it.

What are the various forms of exposure therapy?

The main form of exposure therapy in use today is exposure to the real-life situation that frightens you (*exposure in vivo*). If you do not have ready access to the real thing, such as with a phobia of thunderstorms, then you may substitute photographs, models, films, or audiovisual tapes of the object or situation that frightens you. Another alternative is to simply imagine the feared situation vividly in your mind's eye: *exposure in fantasy*.

A gradual form of exposure is called *desensitization*. In this procedure you progress very slowly, beginning with exposure to an object or situation that is only a little bit frightening and gradually confronting situations that are more feared. This is different from the form of exposure called *flooding*, in which you are exposed to the most frightening object or situation from the very beginning. Desensitization is like wading in from the shallow end of the swimming pool, and flooding is like diving into the deep end. Both flooding and desensitization can be done with objects or situations from either real-life (in vivo) or fantasy. Flooding in fantasy is sometimes called *implosion*. In fact there are about 60 different names given to various forms of exposure, but the underlying principle is the same for all of them.

One technique that has often been recommended as part of exposure is relaxation exercises, but in our experience these are usually unnecessary. After much research it has been found that relaxation exercises don't really contribute anything to exposure for most people. But relaxation certainly does no harm, and some people find that it can help them to continue facing their anxiety without escape and without carrying out rituals.

BEHAVIOR THERAPY OF PARTICULAR DISORDERS

Agoraphobia

Jean was a married woman of 40 who had been agoraphobic for 15 years. In the year before treatment, Jean had not been able to leave her house at all without her husband. Before starting treatment she agreed with her therapist that there were two main targets she wished to achieve by the end of the initial treatment: crossing a moderately busy street alone and shopping in small stores nearby without crossing streets.

Treatment began with Jean's therapist taking her to the road just outside the hospital and helping her across. They repeated this several times, the therapist gradually leaving her side, staying first a few yards away and then further away while Jean did the crossing on her own as he watched. By the end of the first 90-minute treatment session, Jean was very pleased and surprised with her own performance and at how much calmer she felt compared with the first time she had crossed the road. She was asked to practice crossing roads of similar traffic density near her home before she attended the next session.

In the following session Jean made similar trips outside the hospital, but this time more trips were made alone and further from the hospital. She reported that she still panicked in streets and had to hold on to people, and that

during lunchtime at work a friend helped her cross the road.
Jean was asked now to go to work and return by bus alone
instead of relying on rides from friends. She and the therapist
worked out a program of longer walks and bus journeys to
complete between sessions. By the end of the eighth session
Jean was discharged from treatment but asked to continue to
set targets for herself to accomplish and to return six months
later so that the therapist could measure her progress. Jean's
improvement was striking six months after leaving treatment,
and she became able to do even more things alone.

Social Phobia

Emma was a single 26-year-old secretary who for seven
years had been anxious when she had to eat or drink in
company. Emma's anxiety began when she was working in
a busy office. After a friend mentioned how she had felt
nervous taking tea to her boss, Emma was asked to serve tea
to a group of accountants. Emma panicked, and the group
laughed at her. Thereafter she avoided eating and especially
drinking in public. She was even uneasy drinking tea or
coffee in the office with her friends. When Emma attended a
social event, such as a meal with her friend, she could make
the anxiety bearable only by having a stiff drink of vodka
beforehand, and during the meal or party she would sneak
out to the ladies' room with a concealed bottle of vodka.
Public places where she was not expected to drink, such as
the cinema, did not bother her.

Emma was treated in six sessions, during which she was
continually persuaded to do those things that frightened her.
During treatment sessions with her therapist, she drank
coffee in a busy cafe for 30 minutes, then soft drinks in a
moderately busy pub, and thereafter soft drinks in a very

busy pub. At the end of that session, her therapist allowed her one alcoholic drink.

Between sessions Emma was asked to attend a restaurant every day for lunch and coffeehouses each afternoon, and to stay there until her anxiety had diminished. On her final (sixth) treatment session, she was asked to spend 2½ hours making trays of tea and coffee in a hospital outpatient department and to carry these to staff and patients all over the building. She found this difficult at first, but it became easier as time wore on. Shortly after this she made her first panic-free visit to pubs and parties with friends. Her self-confidence soared, her spirits rose, and she no longer avoided any special situations. When last seen, at six months after completing therapy, Emma retained her improvement.

Exposure Treatment Plus Social Role Playing. Sometimes treatment can be a bit more complicated when *role playing techniques* have to be used, as in the case of Pat, a 19-year-old office worker who had social fears for four years. Pat was markedly anxious if she visited people in their homes and could not eat a meal with them. She could eat a meal in a restaurant or office cafeteria when alone but not while sharing the table with someone else. She had always been shy and reserved, and her social life was limited. She and her boyfriend visited each other's homes once a week but no meal was taken in either place.

Before treatment Pat agreed with the therapist that she wanted to achieve the target of eating a meal with three other friends, and of eating a meal at her boyfriend's home. To begin the treatment, Pat lunched with her therapist; she felt very anxious at the start of the meal, but by the end of it, an hour later, was feeling very comfortable. The next time she had a meal with the therapist, she felt comfortable but was still unable thereafter to have a meal with her boyfriend. It was not practical to bring her boyfriend into treatment, so Pat was asked to imagine the situation and experience it in her mind's eye. She was asked to describe to the therapist in great detail how she was picturing herself having a meal with her boyfriend. The therapist prompted her flow of talk when she hesitated.

Pat was then taught by role playing to assert herself when necessary. In a series of "playlets" to overcome her shyness, the therapist pretended to be a shop assistant, and Pat was asked to act the part of a customer returning defective goods. This was recorded on videotape and played back to show her how she had performed. The therapist coached her in what to say as a disgruntled customer, and they played the same parts once more. They then switched roles, the therapist playing the customer and Pat playing the salesperson, to give her the experience of the other side of the situation. Other situations were then acted out, such as asking directions in the street from a stranger and refusing to carry out an unreasonable request from a colleague. The therapist showed Pat what to do first and then asked Pat to do the same thing. She responded well to this modeling and coaching and eventually managed to have lunch with a strange man.

At this stage Pat was asked to join a group of five other people with similar social fears. These six people took part in a day-long group therapy session that lasted nine hours in all. When they met in the morning, the therapist outlined the day's program over coffee. The participants then played contact party games, which encouraged them to mix together. In one game, one of the participants had to "break out" of a circle made by the others. In another game, without using their hands, they had to transfer an orange held under their neck to another person. These warm-up exercises led to the role playing of increasingly difficult social situations.

Toward evening the group split into smaller groups to shop for the meal they were to cook together in the therapist's apartment. During this period, they chatted a lot to one another and then ate the meal together. After their initial discomfort, the participants obviously enjoyed themselves and made plans to meet one another after the group's conclusion.

Pat felt that she had gained a lot from the day-long session with the group. All her other sessions were with the therapist alone. After 18 sessions in all, Pat felt that she had achieved as much of her target goals as she wanted and was discharged from treatment. Six months later, Pat was able to eat with her fiancé and his family and had also eaten in selected restaurants with him and occasionally with a larger group of additional friends. She still did not enjoy meeting many strangers but could cope with them when necessary and no longer avoided them.

Simple Phobia

A 20-year-old woman had had a fear of dogs since she was four. She would cross roads to avoid dogs and would not visit friends who had dogs. Although she was a painter, she could not go out into the countryside to paint landscapes because of her fear. She was treated in two sessions, each two hours long. In the first session a gentle little dog was gradually brought nearer to her; the therapists patted the dog and then encouraged the young woman to follow suit. At first she was terrified, cried, and backed away, but slowly as the session went by she acquired confidence. After a few minutes she touched the rump of the dog for the first time and said, "It is so horrible and ugly; the whole dog seems like a head to me." As the minutes ticked past, however, the fears gradually died down and she stopped crying, began cuddling the dog, and said she didn't know why she had thought dogs were ugly before. Her attitude changed within a few hours. In the second session a larger dog was brought in and the same process was repeated. By the end of the four hours of treatment, she did not have any more fear of dogs than would the average person. Six months after treatment, she reported that she visited friends who owned dogs, played with the dogs, and no longer avoided them in the street, although she remained wary of very large dogs. In fact, this woman had gained so much confidence that this also spilled over into another area where she had had slight difficulties, in her dealings with her parents. She had become more assertive with them and, as a result, got on better with them.

Blood-Injury Phobia

Mary, age 29, had two children. Since age four she had fainted at the sight of blood or injury or even when hearing the subject discussed. She was unable to fulfill her long-standing ambition to become a teacher because she thought she might faint in dealing with children's cuts, which would inevitably be part of such work. She avoided films and plays that might include bloody injury scenes. She became ashamed of this problem and determined to overcome it after she fainted in a hospital emergency room with her son sitting on her lap while his scalded foot was being treated.

Mary and her therapist agreed on four targets for treatment: watching blood being taken, first from someone else and then from herself; being able to cope with her children receiving first aid; and getting her own varicose veins treated. Treatment took the form of the usual principle of steady exposure to the troublesome situation until it no longer caused distress (in this case, fainting).

Mary was asked to look at scenes of blood and injury; to prevent fainting she did so while lying down during the first few sessions so that the blood supply to her brain would continue even if her heart rate slowed down greatly. At Mary's first treatment session she lay down and watched blood being taken from her therapist. She was delighted that for the first time she could remember she had not actually fainted or felt faint at the sight of blood. She then had blood taken from herself while lying down and again remained conscious, but she felt very faint when she tried to stand afterward. She took home an ampule of her blood to keep in her bedroom.

In the next session, because of the inconvenience of arranging to see many real-life situations involving injury, Mary was asked instead to imagine these and watch them on films. She described scenes in which she had a car accident and received severe injuries to her legs and, later, scenes in which her fingertips were cut off in another accident. Then Mary watched films of operations, accidents, blood donors, blood transfusions, traffic accidents, and open-heart surgery; once she fainted while watching these films. She persisted in seeing them to the point of boredom. Finally she visited the hematology department of the nearby hospital and had her blood taken there.

Between sessions at home, Mary dealt successfully with several small emergencies with her children, and she had her varicose veins treated by injection. Eight months after treatment Mary reported that she remained free of her problem concerning blood and injury, enrolled in a first-aid class, began to attend a teacher-training college, and went freely to films and plays depicting blood and injury.

Illness Phobia

Mr. Jones' main problem was a restricted social and work life resulting from continuous worry about the state of his health. This problem had been with him for two years and caused avoidance of physical work and any strenuous social activity. Mr. Jones also had difficulty leaving the area around his home because he knew where all the nearby pay telephones were in case he had a "heart attack" and was afraid to leave his familiar neighborhood. Mr. Jones was in constant touch with his family physician to obtain reassurance regarding his health.

Treatment was initiated with gradual exposure to the feared situation (carrying out physical activity in situations he had been avoiding). Role playing was done with Mr. Jones' wife to show her how to cope with his panics, and a self-regulation program was instituted to stop the need for the family physician's reassurance and to reduce Mr. Jones' constant talk about his health. When Mr. Jones developed symptoms, he was encouraged to continue his physical task. His wife rang an annoying ship's bell whenever Mr. Jones spoke about his health. Mr. Jones recorded any visits to his family physician and also the amount of health talk each day.

At the end of treatment, Mr. Jones experienced occasional anxiety about his health but was able to work and pursue an active social life without seeking reassurance from his family or physician.

Obsessive-Compulsive Disorder

Sample case histories for people with Obsessive-Compulsive Disorder can be found on pages 59–62.

The main difference in the treatment of Obsessive-Compulsive Disorder as opposed to Phobic Disorder is that obsessive-compulsives engage in rituals, which they are asked to refrain from carrying out after exposure. When exposure treatment was first used, some therapists would supervise patients around the clock to prevent them from ritualizing, but it has been found that the critical thing is for sufferers to monitor themselves rather than to have a permanent supervisor watching them. Their *response prevention,* as it is called, is self-imposed. This is usually not accomplished all at once, but instead is done gradually. As an example, a person who washes his hands 100 times daily would set a target of 90 washes a day the first week, 80 the week after, 70 the week after that, and so on.

Anxiety States

Behavior therapy has not yet been applied systematically to people with either Panic Disorder or Generalized Anxiety Disorder. In theory it should be possible for such people to be treated by exposure in fantasy. They could be asked to imagine themselves as being anxious without cause, with their heart beating rapidly, sweating, trembling, and the like, for long periods until they got bored with the experience. Very preliminary study suggests that this technique may be useful for these anxiety states, but much more work is needed before this approach can be recommended with confidence.

Chronic Post-Traumatic Stress Disorder

Some clinicians report that exposure therapy appears to be ineffective for chronic Post-Traumatic Stress Disorder.

Some anecdotes suggest that exposure helps the phobic component of chronic Post-Traumatic Stress Disorder, but much more scientific investigation would be required before definitive conclusions could be drawn. Currently we don't know the effects of behavior therapy on this disorder with any certainty. The research remains to be done.

Acute Post-Traumatic Stress Disorder

After experiencing a substantial traumatic stress that would evoke significant symptoms of distress in almost everyone (military combat, rape or assault, floods, large fires, or accidents involving serious physical injury), some people develop Post-Traumatic Stress Disorder. Characteristics include reexperiencing of the trauma in the form of flashbacks, nightmares, or feeling or acting as if the traumatic event were reoccurring; loss of interest in the external world; symptoms of exaggerated alertness, often shown by an unusual startle response; sleep problems; difficulty with concentrating or with memory; and attempts to avoid activities that remind the person of the traumatic event because symptoms are increased by such encounters.

With the acute form of Post-Traumatic Stress Disorder, there is good evidence, from military experiences from the Second World War onward, that rapid reexposure to the settings in which the trauma occurred is most helpful in quickly alleviating acute Post-Traumatic Stress Disorder and preventing the development of chronic Post-Traumatic Stress Disorder. Avoiding the traumatic situation clearly delays recovery and is associated with a significant risk of developing chronic Post-Traumatic Stress Disorder, which can last for decades and is difficult to treat.

Exposure need not be sudden or more than the individual

can tolerate, but it should be frequent and include as many aspects of the traumatic situation as is feasible and safe. Thus, a person involved in an automobile accident in which someone else has been killed should return to driving as quickly as possible and be encouraged to drive over the same route he or she had followed when the accident occurred. This "treatment" should be continued until distress associated with driving diminishes markedly.

In battle situations, soldiers who are so psychologically traumatized by intense combat that they cannot function are routinely removed from the firing line to a nearby aid station. Those who are returned to their combat units within 72 hours after sleep, food, and an opportunity to talk about their experience almost never develop chronic Post-Traumatic Stress Disorder. If the same soldiers are evacuated to hospitals far behind the lines, they are much more likely to develop the chronic form of Post-Traumatic Stress Disorder and suffer lasting disability. The adage about climbing right back on the horse that has thrown you clearly applies to a wide range of traumatic experiences.

FACTORS THAT CAN INTERFERE WITH BEHAVIOR THERAPY

The chief reason for failure of behavior therapy is not carrying out exposure treatment with sufficient thoroughness. The therapy takes time, and its application must be systematic until most of the fear has been reduced to tolerable levels or less. If you feel that you don't really have the time or energy to do it, don't try to begin. Half-hearted attempts might simply discourage you from trying it properly when you eventually do have the time and energy to get on with it, and you may be tempted to escape prematurely from the feared situation, which could even sensitize you further, causing greater difficulty. So do it properly if you are going to do it at all. If in doubt, seek professional help.

Excessive use of sedative drugs or alcohol is the second most common cause of failure. While carrying out exposure, you should not be taking more than about 5 milligrams of diazepam (Valium) or its equivalent (see Table 9 on pages 144–145) a day, and no more than one can of beer, one glass of wine, or one mixed drink a day. You must concentrate on the exposure tasks and not be befuddled during them. If you are using high doses of drugs or alcohol, then you should withdraw them very slowly over a couple of months until your level is low enough to start exposure. Of course, in the case of prescription drugs, you should consult your physician before changing your dosage. If you have difficulty reducing your use of prescription drugs or alcohol, you should discuss this problem with a physician and attempt to resolve it before attempting behavior therapy of an Anxiety Disorder.

Interpersonal and family problems can also interfere with behavior therapy. It is best to ask trustworthy family members to serve as cotherapists if they can be recruited willingly. If you are having conflicts with your family, it is probably best to seek professional help to try to improve that situation if you think it will get in the way of your treatment. However, such a step is usually not essential.

Severe depression interferes with motivation to carry out treatment. If you feel that life is not worth living, that you have no future at all, and that everything seems black, then you should certainly seek professional help. Mild depression does not interfere with behavior therapy.

The main side effect of exposure therapy is anxiety while in contact with things that bring on the phobia or rituals. We have already explained that this is not serious and nearly always subsides in time. You may have a couple of nightmares in the first couple of nights of therapy, but these will soon pass.

COMPARE BENEFITS AND COSTS OF BEHAVIOR AND DRUG TREATMENTS

Behavior therapy costs the effort and time put into exposure exercises, and there may be the emotional expense of a fair amount of anxiety during the early stages of treatment. But the outcome of behavior therapy is good in motivated people who are not taking sedatives. In fact, long-term follow-up of phobics and ritualizers after exposure is among the best studied outcome data in the whole field of psychiatry. Few psychiatric treatments other than exposure have been similarly tested four to seven years after treatment and been found to retain their good effects even then. The benefits are great—enduring reduction of suffering and handicap.

Drug treatment often carries side effects, and these may not be negligible even if they are not serious. Research with drug treatment of Anxiety Disorders has also shown that most people tend to relapse eventually after stopping treatment, so they may have to continue using medications for many years, which is a disadvantage. Nevertheless, if depression complicates the Anxiety Disorder, then antidepressant medications should certainly be tried. Except for the different side effects of these drugs found in different people, it doesn't in general matter which antidepressant drug you are given. However, some people who fail to respond to one drug will respond to another. On the whole, the cheapest drugs seem to be just as good as the most expensive. Antidepressants, which are commonly prescribed for panics, are compatible with exposure therapy. Antianxiety drugs in more than minimal doses (5 milligrams of diazepam per day or an equivalent dose of other drugs [see Chapter 7]) or alcohol may interfere with the effects of exposure therapy.

When behavior therapy can be largely self-administered, it is cheaper than drugs, more durable in its effects, and free of annoying and some potentially dangerous side effects. If a lot of exposure has to be done laboriously by a professional, then costs will mount rapidly. Apart from their side effects, the cost of drugs varies enormously, with imipramine costing very little, others costing more, and a few costing quite a lot.

An Alternative View

Clinicians, including the authors, differ with regard to the comparative benefits and costs of behavior and drug treatments. The following paragraphs represent an alternative view to that given above.

While behavior therapy has produced substantial and lasting benefits for many people with certain Anxiety Disorders, it is not a panacea. Many people are unable or unwilling to invest the time and effort necessary to ensure a successful outcome, some fail to improve sufficiently despite intensive treatment efforts, and others do not have access to adequately trained behavior therapists. In addition, the success of behavior therapy has been best established for only some aspects of Anxiety Disorders (phobic avoidance and rituals), and its value for other components of Anxiety Disorders is less established. The patients who were involved in the successful long-term follow-up studies referred to above may have been a fairly select group and not representative of the majority of others with the same disorders.

In Panic Disorder, in the absence of avoidance behaviors, drug therapy has been conclusively shown to reduce or eliminate panics while the role of behavior therapy has not been established. While it is true that the relapse rate is high when drugs are discontinued, they have been used to effectively treat many patients with Panic Disorders over long periods of time with a minimum of inconvenience.

While patients with chronic Anxiety Disorders may relapse when drugs are discontinued, many with short-lived anxiety problems benefit from drug therapy and do not relapse with discontinuation. In this latter group, behavior therapy may be unavailable, ineffective, or too time-consuming to justify the effort.

Finally, while self-administered behavior therapy has no therapist costs, it can be time-consuming, and—for some—time is money. For example, a person with public speaking anxiety (Social Phobia) may prefer to take a single dose of an antianxiety drug such as propranolol before speaking engagements rather than embark on a potentially beneficial but time-consuming course of behavior therapy.

Both behavior therapy and drugs have important roles in the treatment of Anxiety Disorders. An important aspect of therapy is to match treatments and patients in ways that will ensure a successful, safe, and lasting outcome with a minimum of risk, cost, and inconvenience.

7
Medications*

A S described in Chapter 2, there are a number of
different Anxiety Disorders. The role that medication plays in treating each of these disorders varies
with the disorder and the patient. Medications are not
cure-alls and, if used, should be only one aspect of a
comprehensive treatment program. There may be certain
stages of treatment during which medication is appropriate
and other times when it could actually interfere with treat-

---

*The drugs described in this chapter are listed by their *generic names*,
often followed by their most common *brand names*, which begin with a
capital letter. Some drugs are available from various manufacturers under
different trade names, and some drugs are available from your pharmacist
in less-expensive generic forms. Don't hesitate to ask your doctor about
alternative brands for your prescribed medication or about the availability
of less expensive generic forms.

ment success. Also, the relative role played by a drug will vary from patient to patient, with some finding that medicine alone is quite satisfactory, others that it is either not effective or not tolerated, and still others that it plays an important role when combined with other treatment approaches.

Frequently, medication is prescribed for anxiety that is distressing yet not part of a specific Anxiety Disorder. In such circumstances, the cause of the anxiety may be readily apparent, and the medicine is used to relieve symptoms until the problem is resolved. It is important to realize that many people being treated with antianxiety drugs are not diagnosed as having formal Anxiety Disorders.

If you are unsure why a certain drug (or drugs) is being used, ask your doctor. There is absolutely no reason why you should not fully understand the nature of your treatment program. In fact, full understanding of why drugs and other treatments (such as behavior therapy or psychotherapy) are used, and their potential benefits and risks, is a necessary part of treatment. Providing and obtaining this information is a responsibility shared by both doctor and patient.

As with all medicines, drugs used to treat anxiety are double-edged swords: They can relieve symptoms and improve the quality of life, but they can also cause unwanted side effects. The proper use of these drugs requires a skillful combination of science and art, which becomes possible when there is a close collaboration between patient and doctor.

THE IMPORTANCE OF PROPER DIAGNOSIS

The appropriate use of medications depends to some extent on the type of anxiety or Anxiety Disorder being treated.

For example, if your doctor feels that your anxiety is resulting from an excessive use of caffeine-containing beverages, such as coffee, tea, and cola drinks, the proper initial treatment would be the reduction or elimination of caffeine intake rather than the addition of an antianxiety drug or treatment with behavior therapy.

If a person develops an overactive thyroid gland (hyperthyroidism), anxiety (but not phobias or rituals) may be one of the symptoms of this condition. While an antianxiety drug may provide some nonspecific symptomatic relief, failure to recognize the underlying condition could allow it to progress in a potentially dangerous way.

For certain patients with Anxiety Disorder (such as phobics and ritualizers), exposure therapy is clearly the most effective treatment, and high doses of certain antianxiety drugs (such as benzodiazepines or barbiturates) or alcohol may interfere with therapeutic response.

In many patients with depression, associated anxiety symptoms may mislead doctors to inappropriately prescribe antianxiety rather than antidepressant drugs. In fact, it has been estimated that in primary care practice (general practice, family practice, and general internal medicine), more patients with depression are inappropriately treated with antianxiety drugs than correctly treated with antidepressants.

At the same time, it is important to realize that Anxiety Disorders are sometimes complicated by depression; in such instances, treatment must be directed both at depression and the underlying Anxiety Disorder. Thus, the treatment of a certain Anxiety Disorder may include the use of an antidepressant drug if depression is also present, but the treatment program may not require such a medication in the absence of depression.

FOR MORE INFORMATION

In the sections that follow, drugs that are used to treat anxiety and Anxiety Disorders will be discussed. Emphasis will be placed on those drugs that are currently in use in the United States and the United Kingdom, although some consideration will also be given to promising products that are not yet available. Space does not allow a detailed description of each drug. For further information, the reader is referred to a resource such as *Advice for the Patient* (Volume II of *USP-Dispensing Information*), published by the United States Pharmacopeial Convention, Inc. (see Recommended Readings on pages 240–246).

GENERAL GUIDELINES FOR MEDICATIONS

Before discussing individual drugs, a few general points should be made.

1. Before taking any medicine:
   a. Tell your doctor if you have ever had an allergic or unusual reaction to *any* drug.
   b. Tell your doctor if you are pregnant or intend to become pregnant (it is important to discuss the risk of birth defects).
   c. Tell your doctor if you are breast-feeding (some drugs are passed from mother to baby in breast milk).
   d. Learn the name of the drug, its dose, when you should take it, and why it is being prescribed.
   e. Learn what side effects may be caused by the drug.
   f. Tell your doctor about *all* other medicines you are taking (there can be dangerous interactions).

g. Find out from your doctor whether alcohol use or driving will cause problems while taking your medicine.

2. While taking a medicine:

a. Remember that side effects may occur at any dose. Inform your doctor if any do occur.

b. The dose may have to be adjusted several times before finding an amount that will be both effective and well tolerated by your system. Do not make dosage adjustments without consulting your doctor.

c. Be cautious about driving and other potentially dangerous activities. Side effects such as drowsiness, dizziness, or incoordination may occur.

d. If you miss a dose, take it within an hour or so of the missed dose. If this is not possible, skip the dose and continue the regular dosing schedule. Do not double-up on doses—it is not safe.

3. The usual daily doses listed for drugs in this book are meant to serve only as guides. Individual sensitivity and tolerance to medications varies widely, so the effective dose also varies widely among individuals. If you are prescribed a dose that is outside the usual range, you might want to check with your doctor to find out why.

4. Keep all medicines away from children.

ANTIANXIETY DRUGS

Antianxiety drugs are used primarily to treat anxiety, although some are also useful for treating other conditions. Antianxiety drugs are among the most widely prescribed drugs in the world. You may sometimes hear them referred to as *anxiolytics* or *minor tranquilizers*.

Barbiturates

In the past, *barbiturates* such as phenobarbital and amobarbital (Amytal) were used extensively to treat anxiety—there was little else available. Today, these medications have been largely replaced by drugs that are safer with regard to risk of overdose, abuse, and side effects. Most doctors consider these drugs totally outmoded for treating anxiety and no longer prescribe them. An exception is that phenobarbital is still widely used as an effective anticonvulsant for the treatment of epilepsy.

Meprobamate

Meprobamate is one of a class of drugs known as carbamates that were widely prescribed in the 1950s and 1960s. It is still in use today. Meprobamate is now the only one of the carbamates currently marketed for the treatment of anxiety in the United States. While best known under the brand names of Equanil and Miltown, it is also marketed as Meprospan and SK-Bamate and, in combination with other drugs, as Deprol, Equagesic, Mepro Compound, PMB, and Pathibamate. Meprobamate has all of the disadvantages of the barbiturates and questionable antianxiety effects. We feel that meprobamate has little role in modern medicine and do not recommend it for the treatment of anxiety.

Antihistamines

While the *antihistamines* are primarily used for conditions other than anxiety (hay fever and other allergies, motion

Table 4. Antihistamines That Are Sometimes Used to Treat Anxiety

Drug	Usual Adult Dose*	Common Side Effects
Diphenhydramine	25–50 milligrams up to four times daily	Drowsiness, impaired coordination, dry mouth
Hydroxyzine	50–100 milligrams up to four times daily	Drowsiness, impaired coordination, dry mouth

*Dosage must be individualized in all patients. The very old and very young usually require lower doses.

sickness, etc.), they also have an antianxiety-sedative effect. The two drugs in this group most likely to be used to treat anxiety (see Table 4) are diphenhydramine (dye-fen-HI-dra-meen) (Benadryl, Allerdryl, BayDryl) and hydroxyzine (hye-DROX-i-zeen) (Atarax, Vistaril, BayRox, Durrax, Neucalm, Orgatrax). Unlike the benzodiazepines (see below), these drugs do not carry the risk of tolerance, habituation, and dependency. In certain individuals, this feature may be quite important. On the other hand, they are somewhat less well tolerated than the benzodiazepines and, therefore, not as widely used.

The Beta-Adrenergic Blocking Agents

Beta-adrenergic blocking agents are also known as *beta-blockers* or *beta-adrenergic receptor blockers*. The names come from the action of these drugs in preventing nerve impulses from stimulating a special type of nerve ending known as the beta receptor.

These drugs are used primarily to treat high blood pressure, heart pain (angina), and irregularities of the heart beat (arrhythmias), and to prevent recurrences of heart attacks and migraine headaches. While beta-blockers have not been approved by the U.S. Food and Drug Administration for marketing as antianxiety drugs, they may be helpful in certain circumstances.

Beta-blockers include the drugs listed in Table 5. If a beta-blocker is used to treat your anxiety condition, it will most likely be propranolol (proe-PRAN-oh-lole) (Inderal). Consequently, we will focus our discussion of the beta-blockers on this drug. This is not because propranolol has

Table 5. Beta-Blocker Medications That Are of Possible Use in Anxiety Disorders

Generic Name	United States Brand Name	United Kingdom Brand Name
acebutolol	Sectral	Sectral
atenolol	Tenormin	Tenormin
metoprolol	Lopressor	Betaloc, Lopressor
nadolol	Corgard	Corgard
oxprenalol	*Not available in U.S.*	Apsolox, Laracor, Trasicor
pindolol	Visken	Visken
propranolol	Inderal, Inderal LA	Angilol, Apsolol, Bedranol, Berkolol, Inderal
sotalol	*Not available in U.S.*	Beta-cardone, Sotacor
timolol	Blocadren	Betim, Blocadren

been shown to be more effective for anxiety conditions than
other beta-blockers, but rather because it has been used
more extensively.

Indications for Propranolol in Treating Anxiety Disorders.
Propranolol may be used for anxiety conditions associated
with marked bodily symptoms such as rapid heart rate,
palpitations, over-breathing, sweating, and muscle tension.
If such symptoms are reduced or eliminated, a person is less
likely to worry that something bad is happening to his or her
body, and the usual vicious cycle—anxiety, leading to bodily symptoms, leading to more anxiety, leading to more
bodily symptoms—can be interrupted.

Conditions for which propranolol may be prescribed include the following:

1. *Generalized anxiety with bodily symptoms* (see page
   53). A benzodiazepine antianxiety drug may be used at
   the same time (see pages 149–155).
2. *Panics* (see pages 49–53). While some people may
   benefit, research suggests that antidepressant drugs and
   certain benzodiazepine antianxiety drugs are more likely
   to be effective.
3. *Social Phobia* (see pages 32–39). Propranolol (and other
   beta-blockers) may be useful when taken in a single dose
   before anxiety-provoking events such as public speaking,
   examinations, or musical performances. We should stress
   that for most people, a normal level of anxiety before
   such an event is quite common, well-tolerated, and
   possibly beneficial and should not be treated with medicine (or alcohol for that matter). On the other hand, drug
   treatment and behavioral approaches (see Chapter 6) can
   be beneficial for persons who are incapacitated by anxiety of this type.

Your doctor may choose to use propranolol for an anxiety condition that we have not specifically discussed. If so, be sure to ask for clarification and the rationale behind its use.

How Propranolol Can Be Prescribed. Depending on the condition being treated, propranolol may be prescribed on an "as needed" or on a "scheduled basis" (see pages 151–152 for further explanation). When given as a single dose in an "as needed" situation, the amount is usually 10, 20, or 40 milligrams. When used on a regular basis, a dose is usually given two, three, or four times daily in an amount that may start as low as 10 milligrams twice daily. Doses may be gradually increased to several hundred milligrams daily divided over the course of the day. The length of treatment can vary greatly depending on the condition, response to treatment, and side effects. There is a long-acting form of propranolol (Inderal LA) that is effective when given once daily.

Side Effects That Might Occur with Propranolol. A lowering of blood pressure and slowing of pulse are common (indeed, these may be therapeutic goals). However, if the blood pressure drops too low or if the pulse gets too slow, dizziness, light headedness, or even fainting may occur, especially while standing. Uncommon but potentially troublesome side effects include confusion, depression, breathing difficulty, swollen ankles, and rash. Side effects that are more common but generally well tolerated include fatigue, tiredness, drowsiness, and upset stomach.

Should any symptoms occur while taking propranolol, even ones that are not listed above, they should be discussed with your doctor. While some may be serious and require stopping the medicine, most will be relieved by dosage adjustment or the passage of time.

Discontinuing the Use of Propranolol. If you have been taking propranolol on a regular basis, it should be discontinued by gradual dosage reduction on a schedule established with your doctor. A sudden discontinuation can lead to withdrawal side effects that include anxiety, agitation, insomnia, and—in certain predisposed persons—an increased danger of heart attack.

ANTIDEPRESSANT DRUGS

At first glance, the use of *antidepressant drugs* to treat Anxiety Disorders may sound like a contradiction. There is, however, a valid role for these drugs in certain situations as explained on pages 160–161.

To provide a lengthy discussion of antidepressant medications is beyond the scope of this book. Readers are referred to our previous book, *Depression and Its Treatment: Help for the Nation's #1 Mental Problem* (American Psychiatric Press, 1984) for a detailed discussion. Tables 6 and 7 are reproduced in modified form from our previous book to give you an overview of the available antidepressants.

Certain foods and medications can interact adversely with monoamine oxidase inhibitors (MAOIs) to cause dangerous elevations in blood pressure or other severe reactions (see Table 6).

How Antidepressant Drugs Are Used to Treat Anxiety Disorders

Panic Disorder. All of the common antidepressant medicines (see Table 7) and monoamine oxidase inhibitors (see Table 8), except possibly amoxapine (Asendin), appear to substantially reduce the frequency and severity of spontaneous panics in Panic Disorder. In many patients, they appear to block panics altogether.

We begin treatment with small doses of the antidepressant (for example, 25 milligrams of imipramine) each evening and ask patients to continue taking that dose until they experience their next panic attack. At that time, they increase the dose to 50 milligrams each evening until they experience another panic attack. In this way, the dose is gradually raised to the level that effectively blocks panic without giving the patient more medication than is needed to achieve this goal. Sometimes, even with this gradual approach, drug side effects become intolerable or the maximum dose is reached before panic attacks abate, and another drug or treatment approach will need to be tried.

Some patients have their panics blocked with small doses of antidepressant medications, while others require full antidepressant doses (for example, up to 300 milligrams of imipramine per day). If one antidepressant medication is ineffective, another may very well prove effective. Although evidence is limited, some clinicians feel that—in the treatment of Anxiety Disorders—the monoamine oxidase inhibitors (such as phenelzine [Nardil]) are slightly more effective than the common antidepressant medications (such as imipramine), which are, in turn, somewhat more effective than the benzodiazepines (such as alprazolam [Xanax]).

Anticipatory Anxiety. For anticipatory anxiety, the drugs of first choice are the benzodiazepines (see Table 9). However, there is some concern that benzodiazepines may block the effectiveness of exposure therapy, particularly in larger doses.

Antidepressant medications appear to have little direct effect on anticipatory anxiety other than the sedative side effect that some of these drugs have. However, if panic is effectively blocked, many patients learn, in time, that the panics they fear are gone and then stop anticipating them.

Social Phobia. Situational panics associated with performance in social settings are seldom blocked with antidepressant medications. The drug treatment of social phobias is thus restricted to attempts to alleviate anticipatory anxiety (see above) and to diminish the physical symptoms of anxiety such as increased heart rate, tremor (trembling or shaking), and sweating. Beta-blocking drugs (see Table 4) are helpful to some patients with performance anxiety such as fear of public speaking. The use of propranolol (Inderal), the most widely used beta-blocker, is discussed more fully on pages 132–136.

Table 6.   Substances That Can Cause a Hypertensive
                      Reaction in Patients Taking an MAOI

Foods

Patients taking MAOIs must avoid these foods:

- Aged cheese in any form. Cottage and cream cheese are permitted.
- Yogurt
- Marmite, Bovril, and similar concentrated yeast or meat extracts (beware of drinks and stews made with these products). Baked products raised with yeast are allowed.
- Pickled herring
- Liver
- Alcohol in more than social (i.e., moderate) amounts. (Limit yourself to one glass of beer, wine, or sherry. Avoid Chianti wines altogether. You might take more if you are drinking only

gin or vodka, but remember that one drink of alcohol may have a much greater effect when you are taking an MAOI.)
- Broad bean pods (limas, fava, Chinese, English, etc.) and banana skins
- Canned figs
- Food that is not fresh (or prepared from frozen or newly opened canned food).
  Take special care to avoid pickled, fermented, smoked, or aged meat, fish, poultry, game, or variety meats (organ meats and offal).
- Caffeine in large amounts (watch out for caffeine in cola drinks)
- Chocolate in large amounts
- Any food that has given unpleasant symptoms previously

Some patients discover that they can consume small quantities of "forbidden" foods without having a hypertensive reaction. Before making any deviations from these dietary restrictions, you should discuss them with your doctor.

Medicines

While most medications are compatible with MAOIs, those that are not can be quite dangerous. Some medications in combination with MAOIs may cause hypertensive or other severe reactions. Consequently, patients taking MAOIs should not take any medicines, drugs, over-the-counter preparations (including cough and cold preparations), or any other medication of any sort whatsoever without consulting their doctor. Make *every* doctor you see aware that you are taking an MAOI. Ordinary aspirin and acetaminophen (such as Tylenol) are all right if they are not part of a combination preparation for colds.

Table 7. Common Antidepressant Medicines That Are Used in Treating Anxiety Disorders*

Generic Name	United States Brand Name	United Kingdom Brand Name	Usual Daily Starting Dose (in milligrams)†	Usual Effective Daily Dose (in milligrams)†	Relative Sedative Effects	Relative Anticholinergic Effects‡	Relative Hypotensive Effects‡
Tricyclic antidepressants							
amitriptyline	Endep Elavil Amitid	Domical Elavil Lentizol Triptafen Tryptizol	75	150–300	High	High	More
amoxapine	Asendin	*Not available in U.K.*	50 three times daily	150–400	Medium	Low	Less
desipramine	Norpramin Pertofrane	Pertofrane	50	100–300	Low	Low	More
doxepin	Adapin Sinequan	Sinequan	75	75–300	High	Medium	More

imipramine	Janimine SK-Pramine Tofranil	Tofranil	75	150–300	Medium	Medium	More
nortriptyline	Aventyl Pamelor	Allegron Aventyl	50	50–150	Low	Medium	Less
protriptyline	Vivactil	Concordin	5 three times daily	15–60	Low	High	More
trimipramine	Surmontil	Surmontil	75	50–200	High	Low	More
Other antidepressants							
maprotiline	Ludiomil	Ludiomil	75	125–225	Medium	Low	Less
trazodone	Desyrel	Molipaxin	50 three times daily	150–400	High	Low	Less
Available Only in the United Kingdom							
butriptyline	. . .	Evadyne	75	100–150	High	High	More
clomipramine	. . .	Anafranil	50	150–300	Low	Medium	More

(cont.)

Table 7. Common Antidepressant Medicines That Are Used in Treating Anxiety Disorders* *(cont.)*

Generic Name	United States Brand Name	United Kingdom Brand Name	Usual Daily Starting Dose (in milligrams)†	Usual Effective Daily Dose (in milligrams)†	Relative Sedative Effects	Relative Anticholinergic Effects‡	Relative Hypotensive Effects‡
dothiepin	. . .	Prothiaden	75	75–150	Low	Low	Less
mianserin	. . .	Bolvidan Norval	30	30–90	Low	Low	Less
viloxazine	. . .	Vivalan	50 times times daily	150–400	Low	Low	Less

Reproduced in revised form from *Depression and Its Treatment: Help for the Nation's #1 Mental Problem,* by J. H. Greist and J. W. Jefferson (copyright © 1984 John H. Greist and James W. Jefferson; reproduced with permission).

*Probably no physician uses all of these medications, and the effectiveness of some medications (such as amoxapine or protriptyline) for Anxiety Disorders has not been established. These medications are listed because they are all available antidepressants and might be prescribed.

†Lower doses (often one-third to one-half of the usual dose) are used with older patients.

‡For an explanation of these terms, see page 149.

Table 8. Monoamine Oxidase Inhibitors That Are Used in Treating Anxiety Disorders

Generic Name	United States Brand Name	United Kingdom Brand Name	Usual Daily Starting Dose (in milligrams)	Usual Effective Daily Dose (in milligrams)
isocarboxazid	Marplan	Marplan	10 twice daily	30–40
phenelzine	Nardil	Nardil	15 three times daily	60–90
tranylcypromine	Parnate	Parnate	10 twice daily	30–60
Available Only in the United Kingdom				
iproniazid		Marsilid	100–150 once daily	25–50

Reproduced in revised form from *Depression and Its Treatment: Help for the Nation's #1 Mental Problem*, by J. H. Greist and J. W. Jefferson (copyright © 1984 John H. Greist and James W. Jefferson; reproduced with permission).

Table 9. Benzodiazepine Antianxiety Drugs*

Generic Name	United States Brand Name	United Kingdom Brand Name	Usual Adult dose (in milligrams)†
alprazolam	Xanax	Xanax	0.25–1.5 three times daily
chlordiazepoxide	Librium	A-Poxide	5–25 three to four times daily
	Sk-Lygen	Tropium	
clorazepate	Tranxene	Tranxene	7.5–15 two to four times daily
diazepam	Valium	Alupram	2–10 two to four times daily
		Atensine	
		Evacalm	
		Solis	
		Stesolid	
		Tensium	
		Valium	
halazepam	Paxipam	*Not available in U.K.*	20–40 three to four times daily
lorazepam	Ativan	Almazine	1–2 two to three times daily
		Ativan	
oxazepam	Serax	Oxanid	10–30 three to four times daily
		Serenid	
prazepam	Centrax	Centrax	10–20 two to three times daily

Available Only in the United Kingdom

bromazepam	Lexotan	1.5–6 two to three times daily
medazepam	Nobrium	5–10 two to three times daily

*Flurazepam (Dalmane), temazepam (Restoril), and triazolam (Halcion) are also benzodiazepines but are marketed as sleeping pills.

†Dosage must be individualized in all patients. Older patients usually require lower doses.

Post-Traumatic Stress Disorder. Individuals with acute
Post-Traumatic Stress Disorder might benefit from a brief
period of anxiety reduction and/or sedation with benzodiazepines (see Table 9). This course of action is not uniformly
endorsed, and there are no studies showing that anxiety
reduction and/or sedation improves the outcome of acute
Post-Traumatic Stress Disorder or lessens the chance of
development of chronic Post-Traumatic Stress Disorder. The
most effective treatment for acute Post-Traumatic Stress
Disorder combines discussion of the trauma (often with
others who were also involved), expression of feelings, a
brief respite (lasting a few hours or at most two or three
days), and then resumption of usual activities, specifically
including those that may remind the person of the traumatic
experience.

Once a Post-Traumatic Stress Disorder has become chronic (meaning that it began after or has lasted for more than
six months), treatment becomes far more difficult. Common
antidepressants (see Table 7) and monoamine oxidase inhibitor antidepressants (see Table 8) appear to be helpful for
some patients with this disorder. Often, those who benefit
describe improved sleep, lessening of nightmares, and some
improvement in mood. These individuals may continue to
exhibit other symptoms and signs of Post-Traumatic Stress
Disorder.

Benzodiazepines are described as helpful to some patients
with chronic Post-Traumatic Stress Disorder and as ineffective with others. Since chronic Post-Traumatic Stress Disorder may last for years, concern exists about the chronic use
of benzodiazepines, which may cause physical dependency.

Obsessive-Compulsive Disorder. Antidepressant medications have been shown to be effective in about one-half of
the patients with Obsessive-Compulsive Disorder. While

some studies indicate that antidepressants help only obsessive-compulsives who are depressed, other studies have shown a beneficial effect even in patients who are not depressed.

On average, patients who benefit at all improve about 30 or 40 percent. This is less than the 60 to 70 percent improvement commonly found with behavior therapy (exposure and response prevention), but still quite worthwhile as viewed by obsessive-compulsive patients, their families, and the doctors who treat them. Patients often report that obsessions are still present, although diminished, and that they no longer feel compelled to carry out rituals. Improvement is often delayed for several weeks or even months (in two studies, maximum benefit occurred between 10 and 18 weeks after beginning treatment). Relapse is common when antidepressants are discontinued.

Clomipramine

Clomipramine (also known as chlorimipramine, mono-chlorimipramine, or Anafranil) is a tricyclic antidepressant that is not available in the United States but that has been used with some success in treating Obsessive-Compulsive Disorder for as long as the drug is taken. It has been used for many years in Canada and Europe and is the drug with the best documented record for effectiveness in this disorder (although it is far from a cure-all). While it has been used experimentally in the United States and while some patients have access to it from other countries, it is unlikely that clomipramine will be marketed in the United States. Clomipramine is nearing the end of its patent life, and drug companies apparently feel that it cannot be brought to the American marketplace profitably because of costly evaluations required by the U.S. Food and Drug Administration.

Clomipramine is the best-studied drug for the treatment of Obsessive-Compulsive Disorder. In addition to the usual sedative, anticholinergic, and postural hypotensive side effects of the other antidepressants, clomipramine frequently causes anorgasmia (loss of the capacity to have orgasms). This is a reversible side effect, but quite an annoying one for those who experience it.

Other Medications

Since clomipramine is not available in the United States, trazodone (Desyrel), which has a similar mechanism of action, is often prescribed for Obsessive-Compulsive Disorder. The side effect profile of this medication is tolerable for most patients with excessive sedation being a problem for a small proportion. More alarming, but exceedingly rare, is a side effect of priapism in males, in which the penis becomes erect and will not detumesce (lose its erection). This condition can be very painful and may require medical treatment and sometimes surgery in order to be resolved. Published figures suggest that, at worst, this side effect may occur in one in 28,000 men who take this medication and that, in those who experience priapism, perhaps one-third might require surgical correction. Other estimates of this side effect are even lower.

Other common antidepressants (see Table 7) and monoamine oxidase inhibitor antidepressants (see Table 8) have also been reported as helpful for some individuals with Obsessive-Compulsive Disorder, although none has been studied as thoroughly as clomipramine. In general, full antidepressant doses are needed (for example, 200 to 400 milligrams of trazodone [Desyrel] per day).

Since behavior therapy helps a larger proportion of obsessive-compulsive patients than does drug therapy and also provides a greater amount of improvement, it remains the treatment of choice. A combination of behavior therapy and drug therapy often proves most beneficial for patients with Obsessive-Compulsive Disorder.

Side Effects With Antidepressant Drugs

Major side effects resulting from antidepressant drugs fall into three general classes: *sedation* (drowsiness or sleepiness), *anticholinergic* (dry mouth, blurred vision, constipation, difficulty urinating, and increased heart rate are the most common examples), and *orthostatic (postural) hypotension* (lightheadedness or dizziness when rising from a sitting or lying position). Table 7 lists the severity of these three classes of side effects.

THE BENZODIAZEPINES

The *benzodiazepines* (ben-zoe-dye-AZ-e-peens) were first available in the early 1960s and, since then, have become the most commonly used antianxiety drugs. While far from ideal, they are the best antianxiety drugs currently available. There is no question that they are sometimes abused, overprescribed, inappropriately prescribed, and used in incorrect doses for inappropriate lengths of time. However, when properly used, the benzodiazepines are quite effective for as long as they are given—as well as being well tolerated and safe—and they represent a major advance over barbiturates and meprobamate.

The appropriate, safe, and effective use of the benzodiazepines requires active collaboration between an educated

patient and an informed, conscientious physician. While
there are certainly examples of flagrant misuse of these
drugs by both patients and physicians, most people using
these medications are treated safely by physicians who know
what they are doing.

There are many benzodiazepine antianxiety drugs available in the United States (see Table 9), and—for the most
part—their similarities are more striking than their differences. All have demonstrated short-term effectiveness in the
treatment of anxiety, and no drug has been shown to be
more effective than another. It is important to realize,
however, that a particular drug may be more effective or
better tolerated in a given individual. These drugs also have
a similar spectrum of side effects, and all have the potential
for causing tolerance, dependence, habituation, and withdrawal symptoms. Because higher benzodiazepine doses
are often used for panic, the risk of dependency and subse-
quent withdrawal symptoms is increased.

We do not mean to suggest, however, that the various
benzodiazepines are identical. They do vary in a number of
ways, and these differences may determine your doctor's selec-
tion of a particular drug for you. For example, these drugs
differ in speed of onset of action (the time it takes to begin
to work), duration of action (how long the desired effect
lasts), availability of injectable forms (they all can be given
by mouth), and extent of interaction with other drugs.

One very good reason for selecting a particular drug is a
patient's previous favorable response to the same drug. By
the same token, a good reason for not selecting a drug is a
prior unfavorable experience. For these reasons, providing
your doctor with complete and accurate information about
past treatment is most important.

As you can see from Table 9, there are eight benzodiazepine

antianxiety drugs available in the United States. While the usual adult dosage varies considerably from drug to drug, it is important to realize that a difference in milligram dosage does not indicate a difference in effectiveness. In other words, 0.5 milligrams of alprazolam (Xanax) will have about the same antianxiety effect as 5.0 milligrams of diazepam (Valium)—no better, no worse.

In addition to their general antianxiety effect, benzodiazepines may also be effective in preventing recurrent panic attacks in patients with Panic Disorder. While none has, as yet, received labeling approval for Panic Disorder from the U.S. Food and Drug Administration, alprazolam (Xanax) has been extensively studied and is effective. The dose range for Panic Disorder is usually higher than for nonspecific anxiety (2 to 9 milligrams per day in divided doses versus 1 to 4 milligrams per day). Whether other benzodiazepines share this antipanic property over long periods of time when given in equally high doses has not been resolved. At present, if a benzodiazepine is used to prevent recurrent panic attacks, alprazolam would be the drug of choice. As with all drug therapies in Panic Disorder, once the drug is stopped (and this must be done gradually), the relapse rate is high.

How Benzodiazepines Can Be Prescribed

Depending on the circumstances, antianxiety drugs may be prescribed on an "as needed" or on a "fixed interval" schedule. As "as needed" prescription might read, "Take one tablet every six hours as needed." In this case, the patient would decide if and when to take the drug but would never exceed four doses daily at intervals no closer together than six hours. Doctors often use the abbreviation *prn* to stand for "as needed." This instruction is generally given when anxiety is present only at times.

A "fixed interval" prescription might read, "Take one tablet three times daily." This means that the patient should regularly take three tablets daily spread out over the course of the day. A prescription of this type might be written when anxiety is more or less continuous. Regardless of the type of prescription, it is important to clearly understand how a medicine is to be taken. Do not hesitate to ask your doctor or pharmacist to clarify a confusing prescription.

Duration of Treatment

Anxiety is often situational, episodic, and self-limited (meaning that the anxiety will go away on its own once the person successfully confronts the anxiety-provoking situation). If antianxiety drugs are necessary in such circumstances, their use should be limited to as short a period as possible.

On the other hand, there are some people who have chronic, long-standing anxiety conditions that benefit from drug therapy. These people may relapse when treatment is discontinued. (An important distinction must be made between symptoms of drug withdrawal and the return of the original anxiety condition. See the section below on discontinuing treatment.) People with chronic anxiety may benefit from closely supervised drug treatment over a long period of time. Even then, periodic attempts should be made to gradually reduce dosage and discontinue the drug. If discontinuation is not possible, maintenance treatment should be continued using the lowest possible effective dose.

Side Effects

The benzodiazepine antianxiety drugs share similar side effects. Whether side effects occur is much more dependent on the dose used and an individual's sensitivity than on the particular drug chosen. Oversedation is the most common side effect of these drugs—a person may feel tired, drowsy, sleepy, groggy, or woozy. Patients should be cautioned against participating in potentially hazardous activities that require mental alertness, such as driving or operating machinery, until it is certain that drug side effects will not interfere. Overdose symptoms may include confusion, severe drowsiness, sleep or coma, shakiness, slurred or garbled speech, and staggering or loss of balance. Occasionally a patient may react to one of these drugs by becoming angry and hostile, although—more commonly—the benzodiazepines have a calming effect.

While a great variety of side effects is possible, serious ones are uncommon. Milder side effects often wear off after a few days or respond to dosage reduction. Should you have any question regarding symptoms that may be side effects, contact your doctor for clarification.

Discontinuing Treatment

The decision to stop treatment should be made jointly with your doctor. If a benzodiazepine antianxiety drug has been used only occasionally on an "as needed" basis, it can usually be stopped without *tapering*. Tapering is the process of gradually lowering the dose of a drug so that discontinuation takes place gradually over days or weeks.

If benzodiazepines have been taken regularly for any

length of time (even in usual therapeutic amounts, but especially if higher doses have been used), then they should not be abruptly stopped. *Abrupt discontinuation of these medicines can be associated with withdrawal side effects,* which may include insomnia, irritability, nervousness, shakiness, confusion, cramps, and, rarely, seizures (convulsions or fits). At times, withdrawal side effects may be mistaken for the return of the original anxiety condition resulting in the unnecessary continuation of drug treatment.

Withdrawal side effects can be minimized or eliminated by gradual discontinuation, which we feel is a good practice with all drugs that affect the central nervous system (the brain and the spinal cord). For example, with alprazolam (Xanax), discontinuation should take place at a rate no greater than 1 milligram per week. A patient taking 4 milligram per day during a fourth week prior to total one week, 2 milligrams per day the next week and 1 milligrams per day during a fourth week prior to total discontinuation. There is no harm in discontinuing these drugs more slowly (for example, decreasing alprazolam 0.5 milligrams per week rather than 1.0 milligram).

Interactions with Other Drugs

Your treatment will be safer and more successful if *all* of your doctors know *all* of the medicines (both prescription and nonprescription) that you are taking. Drugs can interact with one another in a variety of ways, sometimes exaggerating side effects or interfering with therapeutic effects. Examples of drugs that may interact with at least some of the benzodiazepine antianxiety drugs include antacids, birth control pills, carbamazepine (Tegretol), cimetidine (Tagamet), levodopa (Larodopa, Sinemet), isoniazid (INH), rifampin

(Rifadin, Rifamate), and all drugs (including alcohol) that affect the brain. Although most drugs will not interact adversely with benzodiazepine antianxiety drugs, checking with your doctor before taking any other medicine is wise. The specific antianxiety drug that your doctor prescribes may depend on which other medicines you are taking.

QUESTIONS ABOUT ANTIANXIETY DRUGS

How long will it take to feel better?
Antianxiety drugs tend to work quickly, and improvement may be noted within 20 minutes to several hours after taking a dose. The process of finding the right dose for a person, however, may take days or weeks and usually requires adjustment of both dose and dosage schedule. It is important not to get discouraged if the initial result is less than satisfactory.

Should I take an antianxiety drug when I feel anxious?
It depends. For some patients, using the drug "as needed" works just fine, while others require a regular scheduled dose. You should determine with your doctor which approach is best for you.

How much medication should I take?
Although there are general guidelines for the use of these drugs (Table 9), people vary greatly in their response to the same dose of the same drug. Therapeutic dosage must always be individualized. Some people are quite sensitive to these drugs and require very low doses, while others require much larger amounts to obtain the same benefit.

How do antianxiety drugs work?
The exact location and mechanism of action of benzodiazepine

drugs have not been established. They do affect central nervous system activity and, more specifically, are felt to alter certain brain chemicals (neurotransmitters) in a way that results in anxiety reduction. One neurotransmitter thought to be involved is called GABA (gamma aminobutyric acid).

What can I do if the medicine makes me sleepy?

Oversedation is a common side effect, which often improves over several days as your body adjusts to the drug. Dosage reduction will also relieve drowsiness. If the medicine is making you sleepy and less alert, you should be cautious about driving or other potentially dangerous activities until the sedation has resolved.

If one antianxiety drug does not work, does this mean that none will?

Not necessarily. Response to and tolerance of these drugs is quite individual. If one is not effective or causes intolerable side effects, your doctor may switch you to another that will help.

What is the difference between the generic and brand names of drugs?

As Table 9 shows, the same drug may have more than one name. The generic name is the chemical name for a drug while the brand name is the name given by a company to identify its particular brand of a generic drug. For example, chlordiazepoxide is a generic name, while Librium, SK-Lygen, and A-Poxide are brand names for chlordiazepoxide. While different brands of the same drug may look different, equivalent doses contain the same amount of drug. Different brands can usually be used interchangeably, although brands may occasionally differ in *bioavailability* (the amount of drug that actually gets to the site of action in the brain).

Drugs available in their generic form usually cost considerably less.

Should all anxiety be treated with medicine?
Certainly not! Anxiety is a universal experience that requires no treatment unless it substantially interferes with an individual's everyday activities. If treatment is necessary, it is important to work out with your doctor whether that treatment should consist of medicine, behavior therapy, psychotherapy, or some combination.

Can antianxiety drugs be used as sleeping pills?
These drugs should be used only as prescribed by your doctor. All antianxiety drugs will work as sleeping pills (hypnotics) if given in sufficient amount. The fact that three benzodiazepine drugs (flurazepam [Dalmane], temazepam [Restoril], and triazolam [Halcion]) are used as hypnotics rather than antianxiety drugs appears to reflect a marketing strategy rather than a unique drug effect.

Can I drink alcohol while taking an antianxiety drug?
Doctors vary in their recommendations with regard to alcohol. These drugs will add to the effect of alcohol and may cause more sedation, incoordination, and other undesired symptoms. The safest approach would be not to drink while taking these drugs. If alcohol is used, general caution must be exercised, alcohol intake should be minimized, and special care must be given to potentially dangerous activities such as driving. If a person plans to drink alcohol while taking these drugs, it would be a good idea to try the combination at home to see what the effects will be. Finally, both alcohol and the antianxiety drugs have the potential for abuse and dependence, and both must be wisely used.

My doctor still prescribes meprobamate (Miltown, Equanil) for my anxiety. Is it safe?

For most people, meprobamate is an outmoded drug, having been replaced by more effective and safer medicines. On the other hand, if a medicine works and is well tolerated, it does not make sense to change to something else without a specific reason to do so. Your doctor should be able to answer this question with regard to your particular situation.

How can I tell the difference between drug withdrawal side effects and the original anxiety symptoms?

Drug withdrawal effects tend to appear shortly after stopping a drug, reach a peak in several days to a week, and then gradually fade away after about two weeks. Anxiety symptoms, on the other hand, usually increase steadily in intensity as the drug effect wears off and then persist. Recurrence of the original anxiety symptoms should also seem "familiar" or like "old friends" to the patient. Withdrawal side effects, on the other hand, may include weight loss, exaggerated sensitivity to noise and light, and—when severe—nausea, vomiting, low blood pressure, confusion, and convulsions. To minimize the likelihood of withdrawal side effects, these drugs should be discontinued gradually rather than abruptly (see pages 153–154 for more information).

Are antianxiety drugs addictive? Can I get hooked on them?

Authorities disagree as to the dangers associated with the use of benzodiazepine antianxiety drugs. It is clear that these drugs have been subject to abuse, that they can cause both physical and psychological dependence, and that withdrawal symptoms (sometimes serious) can occur when they are discontinued. Persons who have previously misused alcohol or other drugs are at higher risk for misusing benzodiazepines. When considering the millions of people who have benefited from these drugs, problems with abuse and dependency are really quite uncommon. Nonetheless, these drugs should be used 1) under medical supervision, 2) at the lowest possible dose, 3) for the shortest possible period of time, and 4) with gradual rather than abrupt discontinuation.

What happens if I forget to take a dose of antianxiety medicine?

Missing an occasional dose is unlikely to cause problems, although repeatedly missing doses can interfere with the therapeutic effectiveness of the medicine and might provoke withdrawal symptoms. If you forget a dose and remember within an hour or so, take the dose. Otherwise, skip the dose and resume your usual schedule. Never double-up a dose to catch up. Your doctor may have a different policy regarding missed doses, so ask about this whenever a prescription is written.

Is taking an antianxiety drug a sign of weakness?

Not at all! Not accepting a medication, or any other type of treatment for that matter, when it is both appropriate and properly supervised, could be considered foolish. We consider Anxiety Disorders to be illnesses rather than evidence of weak moral fiber. To refuse an appropriate treatment for an Anxiety Disorder makes as little sense as not taking an antibiotic for a bacterial pneumonia. Of course, proper treatment depends on proper diagnosis, and often there are routes to recovery that do not involve medication. Individuals may have quite acceptable reasons for preferring not to take medicine; if so, alternative treatments may be available.

Which is the best treatment for anxiety?

Anxiety is a term that encompasses a spectrum from normal states to severe disorders that differ greatly in clinical presentation and underlying cause. Consequently, some anxiety does not need treatment, and there is no single best treatment for Anxiety Disorders as a whole. Even among individuals having the same type of Anxiety Disorder, effective treatments may vary considerably. Usually treatment is started on the basis of what is most often helpful for a particular type of Anxiety Disorder and then adjusted more specifically to fit the response of an individual.

Which antianxiety medicine am I likely to receive?

Anxiety is often treated with one of the benzodiazepine antianxiety drugs listed in Table 9 (pages 144–145). Which drug is used will be determined by your doctor after a careful evaluation. Certain Anxiety Disorders (such as Panic Disorder or Obsessive-Compulsive Disorder) may respond more specifically to a different class of drugs (the tricyclic or monoamine oxidase antidepressants [pages 136–149]), so that choice of drug depends on diagnosis. Newer antianxiety drugs are being developed, and some may be available by the time you read this book.

What about the new antianxiety drug called buspirone?

It is possible that the U.S. Food and Drug Administration will have approved prescription use of buspirone (BuSpar) by the time you read this book. This drug is chemically different from any other antianxiety drug and may be less sedating, less likely to interact adversely with alcohol and other sedative drugs, and less likely to cause dependency than the benzodiazepines. At present, buspirone seems quite promising, although it still must withstand the test of time and more extensive use.

My doctor prescribed an "antidepressant" drug to treat anxiety. Does this make sense?

It may. Anxiety may be a prominent feature of an underlying depressive disorder and, in such instances, going right to the heart of the matter and treating the depression makes sense. When the depression improves, anxiety usually does too. Also, certain antidepressants have sedative properties that may be useful in reducing anxiety.

Another reason for using an antidepressant drug is that people with Anxiety Disorders sometimes become depressed because of, or in addition to, the anxiety disorder. Here, the antidepressant would be directed at the depression while other treatments (usually behavior therapy) would be used to relieve the Anxiety Disorder. In the presence of depression, Anxiety Disorders are often more resistant to treatment; in these cases, then, treatment of depression is quite important.

Finally, some doctors believe that certain Anxiety Disorders respond well to treatment with antidepressant drugs, even if depression is not present. In such conditions, the drugs may work in a way that is unrelated to their antidepressant activity. The Anxiety Disorders that some treat with antidepressant drugs include Panic Disorder (with or without Agoraphobia) and Obsessive-Compulsive Disorder. The antidepressant drugs might also be called "antipanic" drugs much as aspirin is used both for its antipyretic (fever-reducing), antiinflammatory, and analgesic (pain-relieving) properties.

Can I stop taking an antianxiety drug as soon as I feel better?

Preferably not. Just as a decision to start a medicine should involve the advice of a doctor, so should the decision to stop. If an antianxiety drug has been taken on a regular basis, even in usual therapeutic amounts, uncomfortable and occasionally dangerous withdrawal side effects may occur if the drug is stopped abruptly. Also, since some anxiety conditions are long-standing, symptoms may recur if a drug is stopped soon. You and your doctor should work together on a plan to discontinue your medication.

How long do I have to take antianxiety medicine?

The length of treatment varies greatly among individuals and depends considerably on the type of Anxiety Disorder being treated. Some conditions are situational and self-limiting, and—in such instances—treatment will be quite brief. Other conditions are long-standing, waxing and waning in intensity, and require treatment that may be indefinite in length. Regardless of how chronic the disorder is, we feel that periodic efforts should be made to gradually reduce dose and, if possible, discontinue treatment with medication. At times, even chronic conditions do not recur when medication is stopped. If they do, simply restarting the medicine should bring relief.

What about antianxiety drugs and pregnancy?

Ideally, *all* medicines should be avoided both when a woman is trying to become pregnant and during the pregnancy, especially in the first three months when the risk of fetal malformation is greatest. This approach will minimize the likelihood of a deformed baby.

Fortunately, there is no firm evidence that antianxiety drugs (or the antidepressant drugs used to treat some Anxiety Disorders) are associated with a higher than normal risk of malformation (the drug lithium is somewhat riskier), and many women have had normal pregnancies, deliveries, and babies after taking these drugs throughout pregnancy. While we do feel that use of these drugs should be avoided during pregnancy, there may be circumstances in which their use is both appropriate and beneficial. Since individual circumstances vary, prospective parents should discuss medication and pregnancy with the doctor prior to conception.

Also, there are no known harmful effects from antianxiety drugs in children whose fathers were taking these drugs at the time of conception or whose mothers were taking them prior to but not at conception (some of these drugs are slowly eliminated from the body and may be present in measurable amounts even a week or more after discontinuation).

Antianxiety drugs are excreted in breast milk, and while the concentration that reaches a breast-fed baby is quite low, the decision to breastfeed should be made only after consultation with the doctor. It is possible that the baby could be affected by medicine passed on in the milk.

Do children with anxiety need medicines?

Doctors remain properly cautious about prescribing medicines for children who are still growing and developing. While antianxiety drugs appear safe for children, their use has not been as well studied as in adults, and concern remains about the possibility of unknown negative effects on growth and development. On the other hand, certain anxiety disorders can have adverse effects on a child's growth and development, and—in such situations—a medicine can be quite beneficial. The decision to treat a child with an antianxiety drug should not be taken lightly; risks and benefits as well as the availability of alternative effective treatments should be thoroughly discussed with the doctor.

When properly prescribed for appropriate indications (for instance, some studies indicate benefits from using antidepressants in children with school phobia) and when used under close supervision, antianxiety drugs can be beneficial for children.

Can older people take antianxiety medication?
Certainly. Anxiety in the elderly can make life miserable, aggravate existing medical conditions, and even increase the risk of death. Advanced age is no barrier to the safe and successful treatment of anxiety. Because the elderly are likely to have associated medical illnesses, may be taking other medicines, and tend to be more sensitive to drug effects and side effects, the use of antianxiety drugs in the elderly can be more complicated than in younger persons. In general, lower doses are used, and closer collaboration among patient, doctor, and consultants is required. Antianxiety drugs can be used both effectively and safely in the elderly.

How will I feel when taking an antianxiety drug?
Ideally the drug will relieve the anxiety condition without causing side effects that are uncomfortable or intolerable. These drugs are not meant to cause euphoria, a "high," feelings of unreality, or a mental numbing—such reactions would be considered unwanted side effects. As with all medicines, some side effects may occur, but these are usually tolerable and lessen with the passage of time or dosage reduction.

What if I am on a special diet?
There should be no problems being on a diet when taking antianxiety drugs. Important exceptions are the monoamine oxidase inhibitor antidepressants (MAOIs), which are used to treat some anxiety conditions. The MAOIs require certain strict dietary precautions to avoid interactions that can cause

dangerous increases in blood pressure. Foods likely to cause this hypertensive reaction are listed in Table 6 on pages 138–139. Your doctor should provide a similar list. While most medications are compatible with MAOIs, those that are not can be quite dangerous.

One should always exercise caution with the use of alcohol in combination with antianxiety drugs (see page 157). Also, diets containing large amounts of caffeinated drinks can actually make anxiety conditions worse.

Can I drink coffee, tea, or caffeinated soft drinks while taking an antianxiety drug?
The caffeine and caffeine-like substances in these beverages can actually cause anxiety. In addition, these substances may counteract the beneficial antianxiety effect of a medicine. For these reasons, use of such beverages should be quite moderate and, in certain instances, excluded altogether.

Can I exercise while taking antianxiety drugs?
Certainly! Exercise is an important factor in everyone's health and may actually aid in anxiety reduction. Be sure to exercise within the limits of your body and take in enough fluid and a normal amount of salt in your diet (although salt pills are never needed). Exercise tolerance may be reduced when taking a beta-adrenergic receptor blocking drug such as propranolol (Inderal).

Is it dangerous to take other medications while taking antianxiety medicine?
Most medications may be combined with antianxiety drugs. Some, however, can interact to cause serious side effects (see pages 154–155). Before taking any medicine (prescription or nonprescription), ask your doctor or pharmacist

whether there could be any problems. This is especially important if you are taking a monoamine oxidase inhibitor antidepressant (MAOI), since certain medicines can interact to cause dangerous increases in blood pressure or other serious reactions (see Table 6).

What about measuring blood levels of antianxiety drugs?
It is known that the same oral dose of an antianxiety drug can result in blood levels that differ widely among individuals. The procedure of blood level determination, however, has not been developed to the point where it is of established value in clinical practice. If you are taking a benzodiazepine antianxiety drug, it is unlikely that your doctor will want to measure its blood level.

The tricyclic antidepressants, on the other hand, have been better studied, and blood level determinations may occasionally be of clinical value. Blood level measurements, however, are not currently a necessary part of the safe and successful use of either antianxiety or antidepressant drugs.

What if I need to see another doctor or have an operation while taking an antianxiety medicine?
When seeing other doctors or undergoing *any* medical or surgical procedure, always tell those involved which antianxiety medicine you are taking. This information will help ensure that the medicine is safely and effectively managed. Do not assume that taking *any* medicine is important only to the doctor who prescribed it.

What about taking vitamins and minerals?
There is no firm evidence that taking vitamin or mineral supplements is useful in treating Anxiety Disorders. In fact, extremely large doses of certain vitamins can actually cause anxiety symptoms. For example, arctic explorers who ate

polar bear liver (which is very high in vitamin A) had symptoms that included headache and irritability. Chronic dietary supplementation of large amounts of vitamin A and folic acid can cause anxiety-like symptoms.

If you choose to take a vitamin or mineral product as a dietary supplement, no adverse reactions would be expected with antianxiety drugs. In rare instances, vitamin deficiencies may occur that include anxiety symptoms among their clinical manifestations. Replacing the deficient vitamin(s) would be expected to relieve such symptoms.

Does it have to be either behavior therapy or medicine for the treatment of my Anxiety Disorder?

Not at all. Some of the most successful treatment programs involve a combination of behavior therapy and medicine. While certain anxiety conditions respond well to either behavior therapy or medication—some respond to behavior therapy but not to medication and some respond to medication but not to behavior therapy—a combined approach can be the most effective. In addition to behavior therapy for specific Anxiety Disorders (see Chapter 6), supportive therapy (see pages 175–176) should always accompany the use of an antianxiety drug. We feel that therapists need to be flexible in their treatment approach.

How safe are antianxiety drugs?

When used as directed, these drugs are quite safe. Nevertheless, any medicine can cause problems, and you will want to work closely with your doctor to minimize the possibility of difficulties. Excessive amounts of antianxiety drugs can be dangerous, and certain individuals are quite sensitive to the usual therapeutic amounts.

Will an antianxiety medicine affect my sex life?

Usually antianxiety drugs cause no change in sexual function. If excessive anxiety is interfering with sexual function, anxiety reduction brought about by a medicine may actually restore function to normal. Rarely, antianxiety drugs can lower sex drive or even cause temporary impotence or failure of ejaculation in males or loss of orgasm in females. Should this occur, reducing the dose, stopping the drug, or changing medications will bring relief. Since drug-induced sexual dysfunction is easily treated if recognized, it is important that you discuss these matters with your doctor, even if your doctor is not the first to bring them up.

Antidepressant drugs used for their antianxiety properties are much more likely to cause problems with sexual functioning.

What if medication side effects are severe?
Severe side effects usually mean that the drug dose is too high for the individual. Severe side effects are uncommon with therapeutic doses, but some people are unusually sensitive to these drugs and may have difficulty tolerating usual amounts. If your side effects are primarily troublesome, it is best to stop taking the medicine and promptly discuss this with your doctor. Frequently a simple adjustment of dose or dosage schedule is all that is needed to minimize side effects. At other times, a different antianxiety drug may be better tolerated.

Are there any long-term side effects from antianxiety medicine?
These drugs have been used for long periods of time in many individuals without evidence of long-term side effects. Nonetheless, physicians remain concerned that any drug used for long periods of time could produce unwanted effects that are presently unknown or unrecognized. Conse-

quently, physicians should periodically evaluate their patients with regard to the continued need for a drug and the appearance of new side effects, and to inform them of any new knowledge about the medicine they are taking.

Medicine has not been effective in treating my Anxiety Disorder. What else can be done?

Unfortunately, no treatment is 100 percent effective. When an illness is resistant to conventional treatments, do not assume that it is incurable. At such times, a doctor should reevaluate the patient to be sure the diagnosis is correct. A second opinion (consultation) may also be quite valuable. A disorder that is unresponsive to conventional medicines may be better treated with behavior therapy or a combination of drug and nondrug approaches. There are a number of medicines that are less well established for Anxiety Disorders yet that show some promise in experimental studies. Your doctor may choose to use such a drug (with your informed consent). Some of these drugs are already marketed in the United States for other indications (such as clonazepam [Clonopin], clonidine [Catapres], and propranolol [Inderal]), while others are available only for experimental purposes (adinazolam, buspirone [BuSpar], clomipramine [Anafranil]). Investigations into more effective treatments for Anxiety Disorders are proceeding at a rapid pace. Very rarely, psychosurgery (see page 181) may be recommended when anxiety is chronic and extreme and other treatments have been ineffective.

8
Psychotherapy

EVERYONE is aware of very anxious people who have talked with ministers, friends, neighbors, teachers, advisors, mentors, counselors, physicians, or psychotherapists and gained a remarkable measure of relief. Those who have the ability to listen—and more importantly the ability to hear and understand what they have heard in some meaningful way, to explain that meaning, and to empathize and support the anxious person—can often provide substantial help. There is little objective evidence to differentiate the effectiveness of one kind of counseling psychotherapy from another for the treatment of anxiety brought on by life's vicissitudes. In fact, there are more than 100 specific named psychotherapies. We feel that many of the psychotherapies offered provide some therapeutic benefit; however, it has not been scientifically shown that this benefit is based on the specific factors or mechanisms its supporters and adherents claim. More probably, relief results from nonspecific factors such as warmth, empathy, positive regard, encouragement, reassurance, forgiveness, simply attending sessions, belief in treatment, and expectation of success, which are common to most forms of treatment.

Psychotherapies are sometimes referred to as "talk therapy." Patients and their therapists discuss the experiences patients have had and are having, important relationships and future goals, as well as the feelings, thoughts, and behaviors they produce.

Although psychotherapies are less effective for the more severe and discrete Anxiety Disorders discussed in this book, they can be helpful in improving relationships or thinking patterns that contribute to or coexist with the Anxiety Disorder. General support of patients with Anxiety Disorders is always of benefit (although it is important that avoidance not be encouraged) and may sustain them through their suffering even if other treatments are ineffective.

Most psychotherapies derive their theoretical bases from psychoanalytic psychotherapy, which is briefly reviewed here because of its historical importance. Behavior therapy, or behavioral psychotherapy as it is sometimes called, was discussed in Chapter 6.

PSYCHOANALYTIC THERAPY

Although it is difficult to describe psychoanalysis in a way that would satisfy the several competing schools of psychoanalytic theory and practice, a brief overview may be of interest to the reader.

According to psychoanalytic theory, anxiety is seen as an emotion of the *ego* (the part of our mental apparatus that balances the impulses and demands of our child-like *id*, the stern and punitive controls of our parent-like *superego*, and external reality). Anxiety is also seen as the key indication of hidden psychological conflict. Anxiety occurring in an analytic session points to conflicts and problems needing attention. Patients may be instructed to use *free association*, in which they talk about whatever thoughts or feelings come to mind, without censoring or holding them back. When anxiety emerges in the context of free association, this signals the analyst that further exploration is needed.

Patients use various *psychological defenses* to keep emotionally charged and conflictual materials at less conscious levels, and the psychoanalyst uses his or her extensive training and experience to identify and reduce these defensive barriers so that unconscious materials may be brought into the open. Once they are available to the patient and analyst, these previously unconscious thoughts and feelings provide guidance to basic underlying conflicts and permit the analyst to form and deliver an *interpretation*, which makes the conflict clear to the patient. Ideally, once this process has occurred, the patient achieves insight into the origins of the distress, resolution of the conflict, and— consequently—relief of the symptoms. (It is important to note that this description of the psychoanalytic process is a drastic oversimplification, omitting many important elements such as repeatedly dealing with defense mechanisms, making manifest connections between childhood conflicts and present problems, and the representation of conflicts in the *transference* relationship with the psychoanalyst.)

This elegant theory derives its origins from Sigmund Freud. The study and practice of psychoanalytic therapy is an engaging and stimulating intellectual discipline requiring years of training before candidates graduate from analytic institutes. Many other psychotherapies are derived from psychoanalytic theory, and although training is usually shorter, they all involve an extensive curriculum and period of study.

PSYCHOANALYSIS IN CONTEMPORARY PSYCHIATRY

Richard Asher, speaking to the British Psychological Society in 1955, provided a meaningful commentary on the psychiatry of his day, in which psychoanalysis enjoyed a much greater emphasis than it does today:

> Psychiatry seems to me to differ from medicine in having a closer resemblance to religion. Beliefs and dogmas are promulgated by certain masters—Freud, Adler, Jung, and so on—and these ideas are believed more from reverence of their originator than from repeated experimental observation. Secondly, the language of psychiatry, like that of religion, is often . . . esoteric and concerns itself with concepts and abstractions whose exact meaning is less precisely comprehended than are the majority of medical concepts. . . . Although much wisdom is written by psychiatrists, the nature of the subject and its language make it hard for the ordinary doctor (and patient) to distinguish the profound from the profuse.

Although the present emphasis in much of the field of psychiatry has shifted away from Freudian psychoanalysis, we are still approached by patients with Phobic and Obsessive-Compulsive Disorders who have received (and some who continue to receive) psychoanalytic and psychodynamic treatment over a period of many years without relief of distress or improvement in functioning, even though effective behavior and drug therapies are available.

You might wonder why some people with Anxiety Disorders continue to seek relief in psychoanalysis, given the absence of scientific evidence for the effectiveness of psychoanalysis in the treatment of Anxiety Disorders, and given the evidence that other treatments have been shown to be effective. In our view, it is because we all have difficulty changing. As William Faulkner said, "What the heart loves becomes truth." Doctors in all specialties often tend to practice throughout their careers according to the lessons that were emphasized when they were students. In addition to the difficulties we all experience in learning and integrating new knowledge and beliefs with what we already know or believe, there is some valid justification for *therapeutic conservatism*, since much that is new is not good and much that is good is not new. One of the most valuable medical aphorisms advises doctors to be neither the first nor the last to embrace a medical innovation. In the end, scientific medicine requires verifiable, objective evidence of mechanisms underlying disorders and of treatment effectiveness. Clinical medicine, however, faces people's problems as they come and often cannot await scientific proofs. Since most disorders will cure themselves over time, therapeutic conservatism (or *therapeutic nihilism* in William Osler's day, when he felt that patients were more likely to be harmed than helped by physicians) is prudent medicine and makes good sense.

Sigmund Freud wrote clearly about the ineffectiveness of psychoanalysis in treating phobia:

> One can hardly ever master a phobia if one waits till the patient lets the analysis influence him to give it up. . . . One succeeds only when one can induce them through the influence of the analysis to . . . go about alone and struggle with the anxiety while they make the attempt.

Although Freud was right about the way phobias are best treated, some present-day analysts forget his advice on this issue. Although we believe that psychoanalysts are sincere in their attempt to help people with Anxiety Disorders, we think that psychoanalysis is an unnecessarily lengthy and expensive way to persuade people to face the things they fear.

DYNAMIC PSYCHOTHERAPY

Dynamic psychotherapies assume that behavior is determined by genetic endowment, present realities, and past experience. Conflictual parts of past experience may be hidden as "unconscious" yet be quite important in determining present situations and functioning. Psychoanalysis is the granddaddy of dynamic psychotherapies, and other dynamic therapies also seek to understand unresolved unconscious conflicts that may lead to Anxiety Disorders. Interpretation of dreams, free association, and exploration of the past as it relates to present problems are important techniques of psychoanalytic psychotherapy. Other psychodynamic psychotherapists may use the same techniques but focus more on present relationships and role functioning. Using these techniques, attempts are made to understand the possible roles that less conscious conflicts play in Anxiety Disorders and to find new ways of dealing with people, thoughts, and feelings.

SUPPORTIVE PSYCHOTHERAPY

All patients need and deserve support while they are suffering from an Anxiety Disorder. Supportive psychotherapy helps

by shoring up defenses, utilizing strengths, empathizing
with distress, explaining the course of Anxiety Disorders
and treatments being used, monitoring changes, and reassur-
ing the patient that improvement will, in time, occur. All
doctors can provide this support to their patients. Families
also need support when one of their members is suffering
from and receiving treatment for an Anxiety Disorder.
Involvement of the family can often improve treatment
results for the patient.

INTERPERSONAL PSYCHOTHERAPY

Interpersonal psychotherapy uses both supportive and dynamic psychotherapeutic techniques and focuses on interpersonal disputes and deficits, role changes, and grief. There
are occasional patients who have obvious marital or other
interpersonal problems at the same time they are suffering
from an Anxiety Disorder. Anxiety Disorders may make
relationships more difficult, and common sense suggests that
the reverse is true as well. Difficult marriages make Anxiety
Disorders, like any other problem, more difficult to treat.
However, there is no good evidence that marital difficulties
cause Anxiety Disorders except for Adjustment Disorder
with Anxious Mood.

When interpersonal problems exist, psychotherapy directed at them is likely to produce improvement in the interpersonal problems. In the one controlled study of couples with
both Anxiety Disorder and marital problems, behavioral
treatment of the Anxiety Disorder improved both the anxiety
and the marriage relationship while marital therapy improved only the relationship leaving the Anxiety Disorder
unchanged and still requiring specific treatment.

COGNITIVE THERAPY

Cognitive therapists help patients by focusing on and changing their unrealistically negative "cognitions" or thoughts about themselves, the world, and the future. Negative thoughts about oneself lead to lowered self-esteem, negative thoughts about the world lead to excessive caution and guardedness, and negative thoughts about the future lead to anxiety, pessimism, and hopelessness. Negative thoughts about normal but unpleasant bodily sensations (sweating, palpitations, shortness of breath with exercise, etc.) may lead to exaggerated and inappropriate anxiety (*catastrophizing*), which then progresses to panic. Specific educational, cognitive, and behavioral techniques have been combined to counteract the negative thoughts so common in anxiety and the behaviors that result from negative thinking.

A number of scientific studies have shown a beneficial effect of cognitive therapy in treating moderate *depression*. Cognitive therapy does not appear to be effective for severe depression. Scientific study of the effectiveness of cognitive therapy with Anxiety Disorders is just beginning. Although it may prove helpful for some patients, whether it is as good as other proven treatments for Anxiety Disorders will require some years to learn. It is also possible that cognitive therapy may exert its primary effect by helping patients do exposure therapy.

SUMMARY

Whatever else happens in psychotherapy, the patient is provided with a relationship with an experienced doctor who has worked with other patients with Anxiety Disorders.

Through this relationship the therapist provides information about Anxiety Disorders and support to the patient and often to the patient's family. Psychotherapists also help patients by providing an explanation for the Anxiety Disorder and by pursuing a particular psychotherapeutic approach in an attempt to relieve the Anxiety Disorder.

There is little scientific evidence that psychoanalytic or psychodynamic psychotherapy is effective in relieving most Anxiety Disorders. At this time, we think that attempts to treat Anxiety Disorders with analytic or dynamic psychotherapy should be reserved for cases in which behavior therapy, medications, or a combination of the two have been shown to be ineffective. Supportive psychotherapy is always indicated and is routinely provided by behavior therapists and physicians who prescribe medications.

9
Other Treatments

TREATMENTS other than those shown to be effective for anxiety disorders are occasionally advocated and tried. (And others are used by custom in the absence of scientific support of their effectiveness.) Not all patients respond to the standard treatments, and some who might respond object to some aspect of the therapy. For example, some people dislike medications or find side effects very distressing, some may object to the structured nature of behavioral treatments, and others find it difficult to accept the psychotherapeutic approach, which is often quite lengthy and probes for conflicts that they do not believe exist. In such circumstances, in which treatments are either ineffective or unacceptable, alternative methods are sometimes tried.

EXERCISE

Several studies—ranging from those conducted on people with normal anxiety in a laboratory, through uncontrolled studies of patients suffering from various kinds of Anxiety Disorders, to controlled studies of patients with Anxiety Disorders or depression—have shown that exercise decreases anxiety. In one uncontrolled study, agoraphobics were asked to run "at their best speed." Running produced increased heart rate, rapid breathing, sweating, and, in some, trembling— all symptoms these patients associated with anxiety or panic. Having been given a physiologic experience of and explanation for these "panic" symptoms, they were asked to enter the situations they had been avoiding and did so without experiencing panic. It may be that all that the exercise contributed to treatment was a rationale that allowed these patients to perform effective exposure therapy.

Laboratory studies of both normal individuals and those with Generalized Anxiety Disorder who exercised vigorously on a treadmill showed that anxiety decreased substantially after exercise and remained decreased for three to five hours.

Several controlled studies of exercise used to treat mild to moderate *depression* have shown that anxiety measured on standard self-report questionnaires, as well as depression, decreased and remained at lower levels after exercise. Whether this was a direct effect on anxiety or a result of reduced depression was not clear.

Many questions arise regarding the kinds of anxiety that might benefit from treatment with exercise, the amount of exercise needed (in terms of frequency, intensity, and duration), and the likelihood of relapse when exercise is stopped. Not everyone can undertake an exercise program and not everyone would wish to do so. Exercise is clearly an experimental treatment of Anxiety Disorders at this time and cannot be prescribed with confidence for any specific disorder. Older people considering exercise should obtain clearance from their physician to check for risks of cardiovascular and other medical problems. Anyone beginning an exercise program should start gradually in order to lessen the likelihood of ordinary muscle and joint aches and pains that are so common in those taking up exercise for the first time or after a period of inactivity. (See Suggested Readings [page 243] for *Running Guides*.)

PSYCHOSURGERY

In rare cases of very severe and chronic Obsessive-Compulsive Disorder and other Anxiety Disorders, where all other treatments have failed, careful neurosurgical interruption of certain brain pathways has been shown to help at least 50 percent of that tiny minority. The neurosurgical procedures are done under exact three-dimensional (*stereotactic*) control so that the surgical lesion is precisely limited. The techniques are surprisingly safe and seldom cause complications in the form of discernible personality change or epilepsy. Death from such surgery is rare.

While clearly not to be undertaken lightly, psychosurgery has a place in the treatment of a small number of cases (much less than 1 percent). We would never recommend psychosurgery until other treatments had been given a full trial and found to be ineffective and until two years had passed during which spontaneous remission had failed to appear. Even then, we would suggest psychosurgery only for patients with a severe Obsessive-Compulsive Disorder or another Anxiety Disorder that is causing extreme distress or disability.

CAUTIONS

There is a substantial danger that patients trying alternative treatments that are new, complicated, potentially dangerous, or irreversible may lose more than they gain. Often new approaches are advocated by enthusiasts who belittle the value of controlled research because it usually results in more modest claims about the benefits of any particular treatment.

Controlled research attempts to "control" for any bias that might occur in an experiment. For example, in studies of medications, both the active drug under study and a look-alike inert substance (*placebo*) are given to groups of patients that are matched as closely as possible on important characteristics such as age, sex, diagnosis, duration of symptoms, etc. The subjects receiving the active drug make up the *treated group;* the subjects receiving the placebo make up the *control group.* During the study, neither the patients nor the doctors know which subjects are receiving active drug or placebo. After the trial period is concluded, the researchers learn which subjects received the active drug and which received placebo. The effects of the active drug on the treated group can then be objectively compared with the effects of the placebo on the control group. Sophisticated statistical tests are used to analyze the results to determine the effectiveness of the treatment. This is called a double-blind, placebo-controlled research design. While controlled research is difficult, time-consuming, and costly, the results obtained through this kind of research are considered more reliable than those from less-controlled or uncontrolled studies.

Novel treatments that are not scientifically evaluated often emerge when medical science has little to offer. One cartoon conveyed the essence of the situation well. It showed a man seated shirtless on the end of an examining table facing a grand doctor wearing a long white coat. The doctor exclaimed: "Medical science has no explanation or cure for your disorder. Fortunately for you, *I* happen to be a quack!"

10

Self-Help for Your Phobias and Rituals*

H OW effective is behavioral self-help for phobias and obsessive-compulsive rituals? Recent work suggests that self-help has much to offer many people with Phobic and Obsessive-Compulsive Disorders.

A careful scientific study has shown that agoraphobics and other phobics who carried out the exposure instructions in this chapter improved greatly and maintained their improvement at least as long as six months after treatment. They improved as much as individuals who carried out the therapy under similar instructions from a psychiatrist, and their improvement was also at least as great as individuals in other studies who received antidepressant drugs as treatment.

A second study, involving compulsive ritualizers, showed that this problem also responds to self-structured exposure

---

*Reprinted in revised form from *Living With Fear,* by I. M. Marks (copyright © 1978 McGraw-Hill; reproduced with permission).

and response prevention, almost as well as when that approach is provided under the supervision of a therapist.

APPLYING COMMON SENSE

We all know that exercise is healthy, but few of us get enough exercise. Yet if a dog needs to be taken for regular walks for its health, we might walk the soles off our shoes for its sake. Many terribly lonely people are only yards away from others, longing for company, but can't push themselves to make the first approach. Yet provide their apartment building with a communal room with washing machines, and they will meet others and gradually develop friendships. We know that we should go for walks and arrange social contacts, but we often don't act on common sense until a suitable framework for action is provided.

To a large degree, behavior therapy is simply a framework for applying common sense to behavioral problems. You can overcome your anxiety more effectively within such a framework rather than as the result of a command to "Pull yourself together" or "Use your will-power," which we have heard all too often. Behavior therapy can do for your conquest of fear and anxiety what the dog did for exercise and the communal laundry did for socializing. But before you read the steps in behavior therapy, you should first determine whether it is likely to be helpful for your problem.

"WILL BEHAVIOR THERAPY BENEFIT ME?" TEN TESTS

Behavioral self-management is worth considering when your problem is not severe, when professional therapists are not readily available, or if you want to see what you can do by yourself before seeking professional help. Not all problems are suitable for behavior therapy, and—even when they are—certain conditions are necessary to increase the chances of success. Before you put yourself to trouble that might not be worthwhile in the end, work through the next 10 self-evaluation tests. These involve questions that therapists might ask you to determine whether you could benefit from behavior therapy.

First, two conditions that are often found with anxiety indicate that you should see a doctor rather than attempt to treat yourself.

Test 1: Are you so depressed that you're seriously thinking of suicide?

If yes: Consult a doctor for help. Severe depression will probably prevent you from completing a self-management program, and serious suicidal intent requires prompt medical treatment, which can be very effective. Do not proceed to Test 2.

If no: Proceed to Test 2.

Test 2: Are you often drinking alcohol to the point of being drunk and/or taking sedative drugs in the higher dose range (see Table 9 on pages 144–145)?

If yes: Either come down *gradually* to less than three drinks a day and take less than the high range of sedatives in Table 9 or consult a doctor. (Gradual reduction in alcohol and sedative drugs is necessary to avoid withdrawal effects.) Self-management is likely to fail if you are drunk with alcohol or sedated by drugs during your exercises. Do not proceed to Test 3.

If no: Proceed to Test 3. You may need medical advice about any physical diseases before carrying out self-management.

Test 3: Do you have confirmed physical disease such as heart trouble, asthma, peptic ulcer, or colitis?

If yes: *(or not sure):* Ask your physician whether severe panic can complicate your condition.

      If your physician does not think severe panic will complicate your condition, proceed to Test 4. If your physician thinks it is safe for you to tolerate moderate anxiety, you can carry out exposure treatment slowly. Remember this when you do your exposure exercises (pages 201–208). Proceed to Test 4. If your physician thinks any anxiety at all might be harmful, exposure treatment should not be attempted. Do not proceed to Test 4.

If no: Proceed to Test 4. Your anxiety needs to be of a certain kind for your program to succeed.

Test 4: Is your anxiety triggered by specific situations, people, or objects?

Answer *Yes* if your fears are set off by particular events—for example, cocktail parties, crowded stores, getting your hands dirty, going out alone, dogs, sexual intercourse, meeting someone in authority, etc. Anxiety related to specific situatons can be treated behaviorally.

If yes: Proceed to Test 5.

Answer *No* if you cannot think of any events that repeatedly start off your anxiety.

If no: Exposure treatment should not be attempted. If you wish to try a more general approach to anxiety, read about the role of relaxation in relieving anxiety (pages 228–231) or proceed to coping tactics (Step 5, pages 197 and 200). Do not proceed to Test 5.

Test 5: Can you define your problems in precise, observable terms?

Yes, my problems in order of importance are (write in pencil so you can amend them later if necessary):

Problem 1: _____

Problem 2: _____

Problem 3: _____

Compare your answers with the following:

Problem	Examples of general statements that don't lend themselves to behavior therapy	Examples of precise definitions of problems that can be treated with behavior therapy
1	I want to be cured, to get better	I panic whenever I go out of doors alone, and so I stay indoors unless I have an escort.
2	I'm a bundle of nerves.	I cannot bear people looking at me, and so I avoid friends, parties, and social receptions.
3	I just feel miserable all day.	I am terrified of airplanes and always avoid air travel.

Problem	Examples of general statements that don't lend themselves to behavior therapy	Examples of precise definitions of problems that can be treated with behavior therapy
4	I want to know what sort of person I am.	I worry about dirt and germs so that I wash my hands all day and cannot work.
5	I want to have a purpose and meaning in life.	I tense up as soon as my husband requests intercourse and find it painful.

Although general statements may be sincere and meaningful, they do not allow you to work out the steps by which such problems can be solved, and behavioral management cannot help until you can describe what you want clearly in observable terms.

If you wish, change the problem definitions you wrote down earlier to make them more precise. If you can now say, "*Yes*, my problems are precise and observable," proceed to Test 6. If your answer is "*No*, my problems are too general to be defined," exposure self-management should not be attempted. You can try relaxation (pages 228–231) or coping tactics (Step 5, pages 197 and 200). Do not proceed to Test 6.

Test 6: For each precise problem you wrote down in Test 5, can you name a specific goal you wish to achieve in treatment?

Before doing so, read examples of more and of less useful goals for Problems 1 to 5 above.

Problem	Well-defined Goal	Less Preferable Goal
1	I want to spend two hours a week shopping alone in the nearest shops or mall.	I want to get out and about by myself.
2	At least once a week I want to visit friends or go to a party or reception and stay to the end.	I want to become more sociable.
3	I want to fly from New York to Los Angeles and back.	I want to lose my fear of air travel.
4	I want to be able to touch the floor, my shoes, and the garbage can every day without washing my hands afterward.	I want to get over my hangup about dirt.
5	I want to be able to respond sexually without anxiety to my husband to the point of mutual masturbation.	I want to enjoy sex.

Can you now write down tangible goals for your particular problems?

Yes, the goals for my problems are:

Goal 1: _____

Goal 2: _____

Goal 3: _____

Proceed to Test 7.

If your answer is "*No*, I'm not sure what I want to achieve in treatment," until you have clarified what you desire in tangible terms, behavioral management is unlikely to help. Do not proceed to Test 7.

Test 7: Will it really make a difference to your life if you overcome these problems? Before listing what you, your family, or your friends might gain if you lose your worry, read the example below:

Agoraphobia
- We will be able to go on vacation together for the first time in five years.
- I will be able to take a job again.

School phobia
- My child will resume attending school.
- There won't be arguments every morning at breakfast time.

Compulsive rituals
- I will be able to hug my children again without worrying that I'm infecting them with germs.
- I will be able to help with running the house and spend time with my family.

If overcoming your problems really will make a difference, write your gains below:

Yes, the gains from losing my worry will be:

Gain 1: _____

Gain 2: _____

Gain 3: _____

Proceed to Test 8. If your answer is *"No,* I can't think of any way in which my life or my family's life would benefit if treatment were successful," then it may not be worth your while going to the trouble of a self-management program. Do not proceed to Test 8.

Test 8: Will you invest the time and effort necessary to overcome your worry?

Will you set aside a regular time to practice your homework, promise not to run away when you feel fear, record what you have done, and map out what you need to do next time to overcome even more of your anxiety? Daily practice is preferable, and if your timetable is already overcrowded you may have to give up some other activity in order to concentrate on dealing with your problem. If your answer is *"Yes,* I promise to follow my program diligently," proceed to Test 9. If your answer is *"No,* I don't really have the time or inclination," your self-management program is less likely to work well, but you may still improve a bit with only limited practice if you are lucky. If you fail to improve, though, don't be disappointed; just wait until you really have the time and energy to carry out your program fully. The chances are that you will then achieve the goals you wrote down in Test 4. If you still wish to attempt self-help, proceed to Test 9.

Test 9: Would your self-management program need relatives or friends involved as your cotherapists(s)?

The answer is probably *Yes:*
- If you hate keeping appointments, even with yourself, and dislike recording your activities and planning ahead. A friend or relative can be your cotherapist and help you devise the framework of your treatment and stick to the detailed work necessary to get over your difficulties. Your cotherapist could regularly sign the diaries you keep, praise you for progress you have made, and help you plan each step in turn.
- If you are so frightened of going out that your family or friends must accompany you everywhere.

- If you have compulsive rituals in which you persuade your family to wash or check things for you, or take over your role in the home, or give you repeated reassurance about whether you are clean, safe, healthy, etc. Whoever you involve in your rituals needs to help as your cotherapist, whether it is your spouse, parent, child, or other relative or friend.
- If you as a parent are trying to help your child over a phobia. Your spouse would then be useful as cotherapist. It is easier, although not essential, if both parents cooperate in working out and implementing the child's program. This prevents parents from working at cross-purposes with each other and prevents the child from divisively playing one parent off the other.

Question: What if my partner isn't interested?
Answer: Treatment is unlikely to help until your partner can be persuaded to join in.
Question: What if I don't have a partner?
Answer: You need to find one.
Question: What if I'm too shy to find one?
Answer: You need to restructure your self-treatment program with the goal of overcoming your social fears and establishing a friendship with somebody who could become a cotherapist.

If your answer is "*Yes,* I need a cotherapist," proceed to Test 10.

The answer to Test 9 is probably *No:*
- If your problem concerns only your own life-style, if it does not interfere with anybody else's activities, and if you don't mind working out and monitoring your own treatment program. For example:
- If your checking or washing rituals keep only you awake at night.

- If your phobia of travel restricts only your movements, not those of other people.
- If your dread of dogs inconveniences only you, not your friends or relatives. If your answer is No, proceed to "Strategy for Treatment" below.

Test 10: Can you enlist the help of a cotherapist when this is needed?

If yes: Proceed to "Strategy for Treatment" below.

If no: The absence of a cotherapist will make your self-treatment less likely to succeed, but it might be worth a try. Proceed to "Strategy for Treatment" below.

STRATEGY FOR TREATMENT: FIVE STEPS

Step 1: Work out exactly what you fear; don't waste time treating the wrong thing.

In your self-management program you will systematically allow yourself to face all of those things that upset you, and to stay with them until you feel better about them. Your treatment plans needs to be tailored to your own needs. If you hate going alone into public places, is it because you're afraid to look foolish, or because you're scared you'll have a heart attack, or because you get dizzy in crowds? If you are upset by dirt, is it just ordinary dirt from the floor or trash can, or is it that you might catch or transmit certain diseases, and if so which ones? If an attractive person makes you go weak at the knees, is it because he or she might look down on you or find you ugly or smelly, or is it because you feel a sexual attraction with which you can't cope?

It is worthwhile completing the Fear Questionnaire (page 94) to see what you might have missed. If you have obsessive-compulsive problems, you should also complete the Obsessive-Compulsive Checklist (pages 95–96). Proceed to Step 2.

Step 2: Write down the specific problems and goals you definitely want to work with now.

You did this earlier on pages 188–190, but may wish to change what you wrote, now that you have completed Step 1, the Fear Questionnaire (page 94), and the Obsessive-Compulsive Checklist (pages 95–96). My problems and goals, in order of priority, are:

Problem 1: _____

Goal 1: _____

Problem 2: _____

Goal 2: _____

Problem 3: _____

Goal 3: _____

Step 3: Prepare your timetable for exposure to the things which trouble you, and record what happened immediately after each session (see example on pages 198–199). Revise your plans each week in light of your progress.

How many practice sessions a week can you promise yourself? When will they be, and for how long? Remember that one two-hour session of exposure yields more improvement than four half-hour sessions. Allow enough time to complete your session properly. Immediately after your session, rate the maximum anxiety you felt (on a scale on which 0 is complete calm and 100 is absolute panic, and on which 25, 50, and 75 represent mild, moderate, and severe anxiety, respectively). Write down your plans for the coming week and record what you did on your diary record of exposure tasks (see pages 198–199).

It might be helpful to discuss your program with a friend or relative who can act as cotherapist, monitor your progress, sign your records, praise your progress, and advise you on the next step. Proceed to Step 4.

Step 4: What sensations do you have when you're frightened?

Check off those of the following sensations that you experience most:

_____ I want to scream or run away.

_____ My heart pounds and beats fast.

_____ I freeze in my tracks.

_____ I feel dizzy, faint, lightheaded, about to fall.

_____ I tremble and shake.

_____ I can't breathe properly.

_____ I feel nauseated.

_____ I break into a cold sweat.

_____ My stomach gets churned up or tight.

_____ I feel that I'm going crazy.

Other sensations (write them down): _____

_____

Read over what you've just checked off and written. When facing the situation you fear, use these sensations as signals to make use of the coping devices you will now decide on. Proceed to Step 5.

Step 5: From the following list of tactics, choose three you might find useful to do or say in order to cope with your anxiety while carrying out your exposure tasks. Circle the letters identifying those you would prefer to use.

Remember to adopt those tactics as soon as you are aware of the fear sensations you just identified in Step 4, because that is when the tactics are easiest to bring into play. Write your chosen tactics on small cards, which you should keep in your pocket or purse. Take them out and read them aloud to yourself the moment anxiety strikes.

a. I must breathe "slow and shallow"—in and out, in and out—and gradually learn to deal with this situation. I feel terrible at the moment, but it will pass.
b. I feel horribly tense. I must tense all my muscles as much as I possibly can, then relax them, then tense them again, then relax them, until slowly I feel easier in myself.
c. I'm thinking of the worst possible things which might happen to me. Let's see if they are so bad after all. Let me imagine myself actually going crazy and being carted off to a mental hospital, or fainting on the sidewalk, or just plain dropping dead. How vividly can I paint those scenes to myself? Let me start with the ambulance taking me away while I froth at the mouth and spectators laugh at me in the street, or (make up your own scene of horror).
d. What can I do? I have to stay here until I can tolerate this panic, even if it takes an hour. Meanwhile, let me experience the fear as deliberately and fully as possible.
e. I have to get away, but I know I must remain here.

Step 3: Diary Record of Exposure Tasks

Day	Session		The exposure task I performed was:	(0 = complete calm, 8 = absolute panic) My anxiety during the task was:	Comments, including tactics I used:	Name of cotherapist if any (cotherapist's signature that task was completed)
	Date	Began	Ended			
(Sunday)						
(Monday)						
(Tuesday)						

Example from an Agoraphobic

Day	Date	Began	Ended	The exposure task I performed was:	My anxiety	Comments	Cotherapist
Wednesday		2:30 P.M.	4:30 P.M.	Walked to local supermarket and surrounding shops, bought food and presents for family, had coffee at drug store	8	Felt worse when shops were crowded, practiced deep-breathing exercises	J. Smith (husband)

Thursday	10:00 A.M.	11:30 A.M.	Walked to local park, sat there for half an hour till I felt better, then caught a bus downtown and back home	7	Felt giddy and faint, practiced imagining myself dropping dead	J. Smith
Friday	2:00 P.M.	4:00 P.M.	Rode a bus downtown and back three times till I felt better about it	6	Worst when bus was crowded—Did deep-breathing exercises	J. Smith

Plan for next week: Repeat exposure exercises in bus, park, and shops every day until my anxiety is no higher than 2. Thereafter start visits to my hairdresser and short surface train journeys.

Saturday

Sunday

Monday

f. I feel awful. I could feel better if I imagined something pleasant. For me that would be lying in the warm sun, listening to the sound of the waves, or (make up your own pleasant scene).

g. These sensations are ghastly, but maybe I can transform their meaning. This pounding of my heart, that could be because I've just been running a race and that's also why I'm breathing so heavily now. This dizziness in my head, that's because I got up suddenly a moment ago or (make up your own transformation).

h. I am so terrified but I will get over this in time.

i. I will never get over this, I think, but that's just the way I feel, and in time I will feel better.

j. I am so embarrassed, but it's something I'll have to get used to.

Decide now which three tactics you will use during your exercises, and the order in which you'll bring them into play:

My coping tactics will be:

    a b c d e f g h i j

    _ _ _ _ _ _ _ _ _ _

(Circle the appropriate letters and indicate 1, 2, and 3 underneath to show which you'll try first, which second, and which third.) For three minutes timed on your watch, imagine yourself in your most terrifying situation, and use one of your chosen tactics to deal with the fear. Repeat this at least three times so that you can use these tactics immediately when you feel anxious during exposure exercises.

NOW IT'S TIME FOR YOU TO ACT

Are You Ready? Now start your exposure tasks and record what happened. Remember, you will feel anxious and miserable at least some of the time during your exercises. Don't be put off by this, but press on until you've beaten your worry. If you have any physical disease that limits how much anxiety your doctor thinks you can safely experience, remember to proceed slowly, pacing your tasks to the amount of fear you are allowed to tolerate.

Good luck. It's hard but worthwhile.

During Exposure Remember the Rules

Rules for your exposure sessions:

1. Before starting each session plan exactly which goals you are going to achieve this time to overcome your fear.
2. Leave enough time—up to several hours if need be—to reach these goals properly by the end of the session.
3. During the session use your fear sensations as reminders to practice the coping tactics you chose. Make sure they are written on cards in your pocket or purse; be ready to take them out and read them at any time.
4. At the end of the session, record what you achieved each time, work out the next session's program, and write down the date and time you plan to carry it out.

And the golden rules at all times:

• Anxiety is unpleasant but rarely harmful.
• Avoid escape.
• Encourage the facing of fear.

- The longer you face it the better.
- The more rapidly you confront the worst, the quicker your fear will fade.

Repeat Your Appointment with Fear Again and Again

Take your first steps at a moderate but steady pace. Carry on relentlessly, confronting your fears, until you find that those things that used to strike terror in you are now a bit of a bore, and until you have forgotten what you used to feel. Although you will have setbacks, these are part of the game, and constant repetition will make them less and less frequent. With repetition your coping tactics will become second nature and enable you to overcome your fear with increasing ease.

Helpful tips from a former agoraphobic:

1. Arrange the expected phobic situations into groups according to the amount of distress that you anticipate in your particular case. Some examples:
   - Going into a quiet street—fairly easy;
   - Going into a busy street—hard;
   - Taking a ride on a bus—very hard;
   - Shopping in a busy town center—almost impossible.
2. Choose an easy situation, enter it, and force yourself to remain there until your anxiety dampens down. It is most important not to run away from the phobic situation too soon.
3. Repeat exposure to the easy situation—the phobic reaction should now be less unpleasant.
4. Select a more difficult situation and repeat the procedure outlined in Steps 2 and 3.

5. Carry on this process with progressively more difficult situations. This should result in generalization of the improvement so that work and other activities can be resumed. This approach to regaining mobility can be very unpleasant and involves a lot of personal distress, but it seems to be the most rapid treatment in existence in which the patient can help himself. We have found it well worth the effort.

If Real-Life Exposure Is Not Possible, Confront Your Fear in Fantasy

Some phobic situations are not readily available for sufferers when they want to enter them. Nature does not provide thunderstorms on schedule for thunderstorm phobics to use in exposure therapy. Those who are phobic of flying will often find it too expensive to fly repeatedly. Instead, you can try to rehearse your contact with your fear in fantasy, while allowing plenty of time for your anxiety to fade. Do this at least 20 times, recording your practice in a log book, and when the real event actually happens, remember how you coped in your imagination.

Don't Let Setbacks Set You Back

Expect to encounter setbacks and be prepared to deal with them. You are bound to feel fresh panic and depression at some stage of your treatment. Just when you think you have conquered crossing a wide street in an agoraphobia program, your next step may fail, leaving you standing at the curb frightened and disappointed. Setbacks can last a minute or weeks. When they occur, you may feel dejected for days:

"I thought I had conquered that phobia, that particular street, yet there were those feelings again, preventing me from crossing."

You must realize that setbacks are part of the whole learning process connected with phobias. Don't dwell on why you can eat in a restaurant one day and not the next. Accept your bad days and rejoice in the good days. Setbacks are especially likely to happen if for any reason you are unable to practice your exposure tasks for some period of time. If you have to be in bed for a few days because of a cold or flu or some other illness, it will be more difficult to get started again, but perseverance will get you over the hump.

Setbacks are the signals for you to try again until you have conquered the situation where it occurred. Setbacks gradually fade once you no longer avoid the fact that they occurred and tackle them instead: "Next week I'll cross that wide street—the one that I couldn't cross this week. I'll have coffee in that shop on the other side."

Although setbacks are inevitable, you can learn to cope with them. Don't be bluffed by any strange new nervous feelings. What will be will be. It is no use being confident on Saturday and being put out on Sunday when panic strikes out of the blue. You have to be ready for it and deal with it, to try, try, and try again until you have reached the stage described by one phobic after treatment: "Yes, I still get the panics from time to time now, but it's different, you know—now I don't have to run away from them. I can just experience them and let them pass while I carry on with whatever I happen to be doing at the time." Recovery lies in meeting precisely those situations you fear; those are the ones you have to master.

As Soon As You Feel Fear, Use Your Coping Tactics

It is important to deal with your discomfort early in its development, before it becomes a runaway reaction. This principle holds not only for fear but for other problems as well. Maybe we can learn from Rex, a large German shepherd that belonged to a psychologist. Rex used to roam all over the town, which he decided belonged to him. Invariably, when Rex was taken for a walk, he would get into fights with other dogs. While walking at heel, Rex would see another dog approaching at a great distance. Without barking or giving any other sign, Rex would suddenly bolt for the other dog, paying no attention to his owner's shouts of "Down!" "Come!" "Heel!" and much worse. Under other circumstances, Rex was very obedient and would immediately respond to any of the above commands.

Through trial and error, the owner found that if he spotted the other dog first, he could abort the runaway reaction by saying, "No!" firmly, as soon as he detected an awareness response in Rex. In this way he was able to lead Rex completely, calmly, and without incident right in front of other dogs. The impulse to attack that could not be inhibited when it was full-blown could easily be inhibited when it was just a budding tendency.

Just as Rex's aggression could be inhibited early, before it really got intense, in the same way your panic can be aborted by bringing in your preferred coping tactics as early as you possibly can—as soon as you feel that premonition of dizziness, or a faint flutter in your chest, or just a hint of goose flesh on your skin.

Learn to Live with Fear and It Will Subside

You will obviously be frightened when you enter your phobic situations. Expect it. Try to experience your fear as fully as possible when it comes. Seize the opportunity for you to overcome it. Don't shut it out or run away. Remember, your sensations are normal bodily reactions. When fear appears, wait; concentrate on remaining where you are until it dies down. This it will do, although waiting for this to happen can seem like an eternity. If you look at your watch you will see that the fear usually starts to lessen within five to 30 minutes—and only rarely will it take as long as an hour—provided you remain in the situation and concentrate on feeling the fear instead of running away from it. If you do run away physically or mentally, your fear might actually increase.

While you are waiting for the fear to pass, focus on where you happen to be. Just stay right where you are until you have calmed down. Learn to recognize and label your fear by rating your level of anxiety on a 0 to 100 scale. Watch your fear slowly calm down as time passes. Plan what to do next.

Take out those coping cards from your pocket or purse, read them out to yourself, and do what they say. Keep the level of your fear manageable, by very slow deep breathing, or tensing and relaxing your muscles, or doing mental arithmetic, solving crossword puzzles, counting the beads on your bracelet or links in your watchband, or whatever else you find useful. Gradually you will learn to reduce your anxiety to a reasonable level, although you will not eliminate it completely for a long time. Learn to carry on your normal activities even when you are a little frightened.

We cannot abolish fear. What we can do is learn to live with it as we do with any other emotion. We can face it, accept it, float with the fear, and let time pass until it becomes manageable. We have to go along with the feelings without resistance. There is no need to be frightened of our heart beating loudly or of our crying. After all, our heart beats and we cry when we are very happy as well as when we are anxious, and few of us run away from the tears and heartbeats of great joy. Bodily sensations do not need to be feared. Flashes of intense panic are bound to come, but they will go away in time if our attitude is "let it pass" and if we do not run away. We need to go with the tide, to tread water until the worst is over. The flash experiences of fright will eventually expend themselves.

Welcome the Worst and the Present Will Feel Better

Many people get relief by learning to imagine the most horrible consequences without flinching. If you have visions of going mad in the street, then deliberately imagine yourself screaming, frothing at the mouth, soiling yourself, running amok, until you can do this in a matter-of-fact way. Eventually these ideas will bore you utterly. If you are at the edge of a cliff and fear throwing yourself off, sit down at a safe distance from the edge and rehearse doing it in your mind's eye, time and time again until the idea loses its power over you. If you are in an automobile in a traffic jam, feeling hemmed in, pull over to the side, continue sitting in the vehicle, and see yourself all crowded in and suffocating. Resume your journey only when you can laugh at the whole idea.

I myself [Dr. Marks] find this device useful on bumpy airplane rides while plummeting through airpockets. I force myself to imagine the plane crashing and killing all of its passengers (myself included), see our corpses, and think resignedly, "Well, there's nothing more to be done, let's just get through this episode as best we can." This exercise stills my anxiety about the journey.

The dramatic relief of anxiety through mental resignation was vividly brought home to me one night when I was on a train nearing the end of its long nonstop journey. Standing near the door was a man from a commercial aircrew, waiting to rush off to join his flight as soon as the train entered the station. To his mortification, the train stopped for 10 minutes 300 yards before the station, and he could not jump out on the electrified line. For the first five minutes he was intensely agitated, puffing furiously at his cigarette, fuming and fretting, swearing, and looking repeatedly at his watch. Then suddenly he said, "It's too late now, I've missed my plane, it's no use." And with that all his anxiety ceased, and he relaxed completely. This transformation appeared as he abandoned hope of achieving his goal, but it was the calm of resignation, not of despair. This attitude can be very therapeutic in tense situations.

SPECIAL TACTICS FOR SPECIFIC PROBLEMS

Worry About Sleeplessness

Maybe you have that common plague of lying awake at night worrying about all the sleep you are missing; this builds up more tension and ensures that you don't fall asleep. One solution is to try and do the opposite. Try to stay awake as long as possible, repeatedly going over what you did during the day, or doing mental calculations, or reading boring books. Eventually, your body's natural controls will take over, your eyes will droop, and sleep will overtake you no matter how hard you struggle to keep awake.

As an alternative, close your eyes and imagine a pitch black window shade slowly unrolling downward. On it you see in large letters the word *SLEEP.* Concentrate on seeing this word on the shade as it gradually winds down. Feel yourself sinking steadily into sleep as the shade comes down.

Breathing Difficulties from Anxiety

If you feel that you can't catch your breath or breathe deeply, try this. Take a deep breath and hold it as long as you possibly can until you feel you are absolutely bursting. Don't cheat by taking little breaths. Time yourself. You will find that in about 60 seconds you simply can't keep from breathing any longer. Your body's reflexes will force you to take a deep breath. Repeat this exercise each time you feel you can't breathe properly. Maybe your breathing problem is the opposite one—taking too many deep breaths. This washes out the carbon dioxide in one's blood and can lead to tingling in the fingers and painful contractions of the hands and feet. The remedy is simple. Continue breathing deeply but simply hold a paper bag over your mouth so that you inhale back the carbon dioxide you have just breathed out. The overbreathing is also then likely to stop. Keep a paper bag in your pocket ready for use every time you catch yourself overbreathing. Or, even simpler, remind yourself to breath "slow and shallow" so that the "hyper" leaves your ventilation.

Anxiety About Swallowing

Perhaps your tension makes it hard for you to swallow solid food. Try to chew a dry biscuit or cookie. The idea is to chew it, not to swallow. Chew on and on until the biscuit is very soft and moist. Eventually after you chew for long enough you will swallow the moist biscuit automatically without noticing. You need only concentrate on chewing; the swallowing will look after itself.

Excessive Tidiness

Ensure that you untidy something in the house everyday if your problem is excessive tidiness. Start by leaving a carpet askew on the floor in the living room. Tomorrow put a vase deliberately in the wrong place. The next day leave something unwashed in the kitchen sink. Expose yourself to increasing untidiness until you have reached the degree of untidiness you want to live with. My colleague, Dr. Leonard Cammer, asked a tidy, clean woman to empty a full ashtray in the center of her living room rug and to leave it there for 48 hours. At intervals she would return to glare at it, but gradually she felt less and less sore about it. Eventually whenever she spotted something dirty or untidy she would shrug and say, "Oh well, it can wait for another 48 hours if need be" (L. Cammer, *Freedom from Compulsion*, Simon & Schuster, New York, 1976).

Hoarding

If you are a hoarder, notice how the clutter in your house prevents you and others from moving about. Think what you can do with all the space that will become available to you when you throw away all of your excess rubbish. Ask a spouse or friend to help you cart away your papers, cartons, or whatever. A charity or thrift shop may be interested in buying some of your hoard. Do not buy any of it back. Make sure you throw away things when you have finished with them or you will rekindle the hoarding habit. At first you will feel anxiety when you have gotten rid of your surplus possessions, but after some days you will be relieved at the extra space you've cleared. Make a resolution to throw away something every day that previously you might have started to hoard.

List Making

If making lists is your addiction, count the number of items you have on your list. Cross out two of these today, three tomorrow, four the next day, and so on until finally you have no more items on your list. You will worry about what you have missed for some days. Accept that you may in fact forget things and realize that this won't be crucial, that the world won't come to an end. If you want to be quick about it, tear up every list you have even if it convulses you, and then resolve never to make any others.

EXAMPLES OF SELF-HELP

At this stage you may find it instructive to follow the progress of two people who largely carried out their own treatment.

Overcoming Agoraphobia

Molly, who was 40 years old, had had classic Agoraphobia since her pregnancy five years earlier. Fears of going out of the house made her give up her job as a physiotherapist. She had hardly been on a bus or train alone for the previous four years and was able to take the dog out for a walk only around the corner. If accompanied she could do more. She was attending an outpatient department every day. She was married to a doctor, and until five years previously she had led a busy social life and loved her work. She thought her parents had overprotected her as a child.

Molly and her husband were seen only once for an hour. She was told that panic would never kill her. With prolonged exposure the panic does not go completely but gradually lessens as one learns to tackle it without running. One has to go out and meet the panic. She could overcome her phobia if she systematically exposed herself to those situations she feared, and she was shown how to keep a diary of the exposure tasks she completed. Setbacks would come, but she must then go out again. As she lived 200 miles from London, no further appointments were arranged, further contact being by letter.

The next week she wrote:

> Since you saw my husband and me last week I have spent three days in the center of Bristol traveling alone by bus. Today I walked around Bristol for three hours. I am amazed how—faced with an open-ended cutoff from home or escape—I coped. I have achieved more in four days than during the last four years, and only feel afraid that I shall wake up and find it's a dream. I would never have thought it possible and it was only your reassurances, that fear will never kill you, that enabled me to take the first bus ride. I still do not really understand quite why the panics are diminished with the prospects of long exposure away from home, but they certainly are. It's incredible.

With her letter, Molly Smith enclosed a diary detailing the frightening situations she had been in over those four days (see pages 198–199).

Two months later Molly wrote again:

> I have enclosed my schedule and I hope that you will be as pleased with my progress as we are. . . . I still run away from anxiety, especially in social situations—e.g., coffee mornings, dinners, and on the bus—where I feel that panicking, with its "sweat, shake, and tears" routine, would be hard to explain away. However, as you can see, local shopping, walking with the dog, and even going to the Zoo are everyday events now and cause practically no trouble. This is wonderful to me—as you can imagine. I rather clash with my phobic friends in hospital who are still undergoing gradual desensitization [in fantasy]. My husband is very pleased too with the way things are going.

After four more months Molly sent her up-to-date schedule showing that she had been traveling freely everywhere and had increased her improvement. A year later she was still better.

> Last Friday I travelled on my own to London on an express train to meet my husband and stay with friends for the weekend. You can imagine how thrilled we all are that my progress has allowed me to travel alone again.
>
> Everyone says I am better than I have been for years, and I have to agree. My whole life-style has changed since my visit to you. I lead quite a busy life now and rarely stay at home. I only visit the day hospital occasionally now, but I do appreciate their help if I hit a bad patch, e.g., after flu, etc.,

as you warned. I still feel very uncomfortable at times, but panics do not depress me like they used to. I can soon bounce back and have another go. I now belong to a badminton group, I have music lessons, take friends for music and movement, love taking the dog for walks, and go to parties with very little problem—quite a difference.

I know we have a little way before I completely disregard panics, but I do feel well on the way. I enclose a copy of my diary, which I still like to keep up. Sometimes I think that I have taken the easy way out again, but I hope you will agree that my horizons have widened.

Molly and her husband were seen only once, and yet she grasped the principles of self-help so well that, without further ado, she carried out her necessary exercises and steadily overcame her fears—not by magic, but by systematically facing each one in turn. Molly did not get cured overnight. It was not easy. She had setbacks, which were to be expected, and dealt with them with renewed efforts at self-exposure. Her reward was freedom from the bonds of fear that had tied her for five years. She has retained her improvement now for nine years—four years ago she had a temporary setback when depressed because of some trouble, but she resumed her self-exposure program and soon regained her improvement.

Overcoming Obsessions and Rituals About Dirt

Now we turn to Sue, who had been terrified of dirt for nine years. Although a nurse-therapist helped her for a few days to get started, Sue did much of the treatment herself. Her program can give you an idea how to set about overcoming obsessive difficulties. The description is long in order to show how much you need to attend to detail. If obsessions aren't your problem, you may prefer to skip this section and go to page 221.

First let's get an overview, and then look at her own description of what she did. Notice the principles of treatment. Face up to precisely what you fear. Never avoid discomfort. Practice, practice, and practice doing what you are frightened of over and over again until it is second nature. In Sue's case the situations she had to practice were those she thought were connected with dirt, bacteria, or poison.

Sue, now 37 years old, had been crippled for nine years with severe obsessive phobias. They began nine years earlier after she read of a local death from Weil's disease (transmitted by rats) and saw a dead rat in the road. Over the next few months there was rapid progressive development of ruminations, rituals, and avoidance concerning imagined dirt, bacteria, and poison, and she washed her hands 50 times a day.

She was constantly preoccupied with "germs" and what she might have touched ("Have I caught anything?" "Have I passed it on?"), particularly those germs that might be connected with the rats. She repeatedly threw away "contaminated" articles, including a washing machine. Her husband and two teenage sons cooperated in carrying out rituals, giving reassurance, and performing the household duties she avoided because of her fears, for example, cooking, washing, and other household tasks. This led to many family quarrels. Sue managed to hold down a full-time unskilled job, as her fears were less marked outside than they were at home. Over the previous five years, she obtained little benefit from treatment, including admission to a hospital, antidepressant drugs, electroconvulsive therapy, tranquilizers, and supportive psychotherapy. With brief behavior therapy that did not involve her family, she had made some improvement but relapsed each time she stopped contact with her therapist.

Sue's therapist described the treatment process as follows:

> Treatment began with five days in the hospital, during which time she was encouraged to "contaminate" herself with "germs" and refrain from washing her hands for increasingly longer periods of time. Despite initial anxiety she persevered with the program and quickly obtained relief. She managed to transfer her improvement to her home, where she began to perform all household duties she had previously avoided, and her hand-washing was reduced to eight times per day. The family became cotherapists, each having specific roles to play; for example, the children had to touch their mother when entering the house and the husband had to stop doing the cooking and housework. Improvement continued to follow-up at one year.

From this summary you wouldn't guess the hard work on so many details that Sue had to complete to get over her problem. Sue's own description of the treatment, which should give you a better idea of the hard work that was involved, appears below:

> When I came into the hospital for five days my nurse-therapist wrote out a detailed program of treatment, which was signed and stuck to my mirror above the washbasin.
>
> *Monday, February 23 (Day 1):* Here is the treatment program:

1. Two handwashes allowed per day.
2. No soap allowed in bedroom except one dry bar, which is to remain unused.
3. Bedroom to be dirtied and not cleaned until further notice.
4. Prepare coffee and tea for several people after previously "contaminating" cups.
5. "Contaminate" knives, forks, spoons by dropping them on the floor, picking them up, and eating a meal with them.
6. Towel in room not to be changed.
7. Not allowed to wash clothes.
8. "Contaminate" hands at 9:00 A.M. and not wash for at least five hours.
9. Bath allowed in the late evening, but only if I keep to the program. (This is an incentive to be diligent.)
10. All visits to the toilet to be supervised. No washes.

I agree to keep to this program.

Signed (Sue)

We then carried out instructions on the program. Soap and my towels were taken to the staff room. I was allowed one clean and one "dirty" hospital towel ["dirty" here means simply that it was used once by somebody else]. The "dirty" towel was placed at the bottom of the bed and I had to sit on it. Then we took the wastepaper basket and went outside collecting muck from around a drain cover in the road and long grass from under nearby huts. We went back to my room and threw the muck all round it. I threw my washing on the floor, and my therapist and I both wiped our hands on the clean towel to dirty it. Without washing my hands I opened my suitcase, handled all my clean clothes and put them on coat hangers and in drawers. I went to the canteen and made tea, putting my hands in all the cups and the milk jug, rubbed the spoons in my hands, and then served tea which we all drank. All the people knew what had happened and that I had not washed my hands. At supper time I rubbed my cutlery on the floor, touched my shoes, and licked my fingers at every possible moment. I had not washed since 9:00 A.M. Before going to sleep I had a bath for 10 minutes.

Tuesday, February 24 (Day 2): I washed, dressed and made up my face, and made tea for the patients and staff, "contaminating" the cups first. Using "dirty" clothes, dustpan, and broom I cleaned the cabins I had dirtied the previous day with rubbish, grass, and leaves. At 4:00 P.M. I went and touched toilet seats and then asked four people if I could clean their shoes for them. After cleaning their shoes I made four people some toast, found two people who wanted their beds made and tidied them. I touched a little girl I was afraid of, wrote a letter to my husband and children, telling them the letter was full of germs, and posted it. I went shopping after touching the toilet seats and bought grapes, which I served at supper to unsuspecting patients. I bought a chemical toilet cleaner, which I handled and sat with on my lap—I was terrified that this would harm me. Before going to bed I had to put my arm around six people. I went to sleep with a "contaminated" towel on my bedclothes, and wore someone else's nightdress.

Wednesday, February 25 (Day 3): After breakfast I went through my "contaminating" exercises—going down corridors touching light-switches, handles, phones, pictures, rubbish bins, soiled linen, urinal bottles, bedpans, basins containing unknown liquids, irons, ironing board, brooms, dusters, vacuum cleaner, mops, bleach bottles. As I was afraid of diseases which might be transmitted by rats, I went to see rats in a cage and touched them, after which I made toast for the staff and touched a lady and her child. In the patients' toilets I touched the seats, made tea, served cakes, and touched the cups. A nurse usually came with me to make sure I did everything and even woke me as I was sitting in a chair to remind me that I had forgotten to make the toast for patients. This I did. I had to read a magazine used by other patients and put on clothes I had worn the previous day and practice touching other people's hair. I washed dirty underclothes in the bath before I could bathe in it. I resolved that I would let a rat run over me, and risk getting its disease.

Thursday, February 26 (Day 4): Completed the "contaminating" exercises involving other people and myself. Bought a book to send my son, and on the walk back to the hospital touched several trash cans and every car stationary at the side of the road. Arrived back at the hospital really filthy, and without washing I then made tea for the patients.

Friday February 27 (Day 5): Completed my exposure routine, cleaned my bedroom, packed my clothes, mixing dirty with clean and avoided using plastic bags. Contaminated myself again before my husband arrived. Managed to pick up the little girl on the ward for a few moments and then went home with my husband.

Self-Management at Home: General Principles
Touch whatever I am scared of without washing afterwards. Instructions for my exposure exercises are on cards around the house and done every day.

1. "Contaminate" my hands by touching garbage can, toilet seat and brush, wheelbarrow with rubbish in it, bird aviary, bird droppings, raw meat. Touch laundry basket and clothes whenever I pass them. Hug my three sons regularly (previously avoided this completely). Fill the dog's waterbowl then touch taps in kitchen with unwashed hands.
2. "Contaminate" worksurfaces, plates, cutlery, pots, and all food before eating.
3. With unwashed hands lie on couch, answer phone, and touch switches and door handles, television and curtains.
4. After touching the garbage cans tidy beds, lie on them, and handle items on the dressing table.
5. Touch the toilet seat and thereafter towels, switches, medicine cabinet, my own hair.

Program 1 devised for March 5: Got up and dressed, put on unwashed clothes which I had worn yesterday, washed my hands, and then contaminated myself and had breakfast after contaminating all the food. Completed my exposure routine, then cleaned the bathroom and the toilet seat using a cloth usually reserved for the bath. Cleaned the bathroom cabinet with the cloth usually reserved for the bath, thereafter handled all medicines. Poured old medicines down the sink. Polished the floor using dirty cloth in bucket usually reserved for the kitchen, and made sure I trapped germs under the polish. Cleaned the toilet brush and holder using the floor cloth and poured dirty water down the bath. Picked up the ironing board and iron, rubbed them against the dirty clothes and with them ironed a "clean" dress. Touched all my clean clothes. Went into town with dirty hands, tried on bras, bought one, walked home without checking where

I was walking, and opened the door with the key (which previously I could not do). Without washing my hands then prepared lunch, hugged my sons, and went to the hairdresser with dirty hands. Had manicure with nailpolish, came home, and had a bath without cleaning the bath first. Used a "dirty" towel for drying, placed the used towel where the family could use it, and put on the dress I had previously ironed and ironed my husband's shirt. Then touched the rubbish bin and toilet. Went to the dance, shook hands with everybody.

I came home, put the dress in the wardrobe next to all the other clothing rather than in the washbasket. Washed my hands and went to bed.

DOES EXPOSURE TREATMENT WORK? THE SCIENTIFIC EVIDENCE

You may be getting impatient at the testimonials from patients. "That's all very well," you might think, and not without justice, "but we all know about miracle cures that can't be repeated. Will it work for me? What's the scientific evidence that exposure treatments work reliably for most people with my kind of trouble?"

In many controlled studies, behavioral exposure treatments were found to be significantly more effective than other treatments in improving phobias, rituals, and sexual problems. They worked better than contrasting methods, such as relaxation or analytic types of insight psychotherapy. Moreover, the improvement doesn't disappear after a few weeks. Patients who improved tended to stay that way over the two to nine years they were followed up after discharge. Improvement in their anxiety freed them and their family from the restrictions that formerly hemmed them in.

One thing may not change with exposure treatments. Before treatment many sufferers from phobias and obsessions have a tendency to get depressive spells. Even after they lose their specific anxieties, this tendency to depressive spells may not change. If and when it happens to you, it can usually be dealt with adequately by antidepressant medication from your doctor.

SELF-HELP CLUBS

Sufferers of many different kinds find it helpful to join lay groups of people who have problems similar to their own, so that they can share common experiences, learn helpful tips about how to cope, and have an additional social outlet. People with anxiety are no exception. In Britain a national correspondence club called The Open Door at one time had about 3,000 members. Similar organizations exist in the United States, Canada (Vancouver), Australia, and Holland. Agoraphobics can club together for outings, help run children to and from school, arrange programs to retrain themselves out of their phobias, and organize many other activities. A few people are reluctant to join because they are afraid that listening to other people's troubles will make their own worse. In general this does not happen.

The important point is not to make the club a complaint or grouse group just out to swap complaints, but a mutual aid society devoted to overcoming problems. This has been done in many ways. People with phobias about eating in restaurants went to lunch together, supporting and encouraging one another as they ventured out together. Others with flying phobias banded together in an organization called Air Fraidy Cats, chartered an airplane, and after preliminary instruction went for a group flight together. Club members can help one another even if their phobias are not the same.

A driving phobic and a walking phobic worked closely together, together driving on various highways and walking in several stores, thus helping both themselves and each other.

Organizations and Newsletters for Agoraphobics

United States

California: TERRAP (the name is derived from "territorial apprehensiveness") (Arthur B. Hardy, M.D., 1010 Doyle Street, Menlo Park, CA 94025)

Maryland: Phobia Society of America (6181 Executive Boulevard, Rockville, MD 20852). Telephone (301) 231-9350

New York: Manhattan Dealing-with-Fear Discussion Group, Inc. (160 W. 96th Street, New York, NY 10025), which publishes a newsletter called *Dealing with Fear*

New York: The Phobia Clinic (White Plains Hospital, 41 East Post Road, White Plains, NY 10601), which publishes *P.M. News*. Telephone (914) 949-4500, Extension 2017

Britain

London: The Open Door (2 Manor Brook, London, SE3)

Manchester: The Phobics Society (Mrs. Katharine Fisher, Cheltenham Road, Chorley-cum-Hardy, Manchester, M211QN). Telephone (061) 881-1937

Northumberland: Horizon (Mrs. Pauline Ayre, 8 Tynedale Gardens, Stocksfield, Northumberland)

Belfast: Northern Ireland Phobics Society (Lance MacManaway, 25 Pennington Park, Belfast BT8 4GJ, Northern Ireland)

Ireland

Dublin: Out and About (Morny Murrihy, St. Gabriel's Day Centre, St. Gabriel's Road, Clontarf, Dublin 3, Ireland)

11

Common Questions About Treatment of Anxiety and Anxiety Disorders

How effective are treatments for Anxiety Disorders?

For any given person with an Anxiety Disorder, it is impossible to predict exactly how he or she will respond to the various treatments that are available. Some people have problems that interfere with or rule out certain treatments, others develop side effects that require a change of approach before benefit occurs, and still others decline to accept methods that would help them. However, if a group of people with a particular kind of Anxiety Disorder is considered, the proportion that is likely to benefit from various treatments can be estimated.

Behavior therapy in the form of exposure to the real fears and things avoided is the cornerstone of treatments of phobic disorders and compulsive rituals. In such people whose anxiety is not a consequence of depression, who are not using large amounts of alcohol or tranquilizing medications, who will carry through conscientiously with behavioral treatment, and whose families want them to get better, over 90 percent will improve substantially and lastingly after exposure therapy. For people with Obsessive-Compulsive Disorder, improvement rates from 60 to 80 percent for behavioral treatments have been reported in different studies.

Antidepressant medications and an antianxiety medicine (alprazolam [Xanax]) have been shown to reduce panics in up to 70 percent of people suffering from them, as long as the medication is given. Antidepressant medications help approximately 50 percent of people with Obsessive-Compulsive Disorder, but the amount of improvement is only about half of that obtained with people who can do behavior therapy. A combination of drug and behavioral treatment is often most effective.

Neither behavioral therapies nor medications have yet been systematically studied in people with chronic Post-Traumatic Stress Disorder, so we do not know with confidence what role, if any, these therapies might play in the treatment of this disorder.

Once improvement is obtained with behavioral treatments, it is usually long-lasting, and follow-up studies over many years have shown that successfully treated people usually maintain their gains. While some people do relapse, they can reapply the same behavioral treatments they previously learned and then usually recover quickly. Medications tend to be effective as long as they are used for Panic Disorder and somewhat less so for Obsessive-Compulsive Disorder, but when medications are discontinued, relapse is quite common, particularly in people who have not done exposure therapy. Relapse is less common in people who are treated with medication for Adjustment Disorder with Anxious Mood and other conditions associated with situational anxiety.

Behavior therapy (exposure) is presently the most effective treatment of Agoraphobia and other Phobic and Obsessive-Compulsive Disorders, while medications play a more limited role by reducing panics and, perhaps, helping people begin exposure therapy. Lasting improvement is expected with exposure while relapse rates are high when medications are withdrawn. Combination treatment (exposure plus medication) is employed by many doctors and seems to work well. For people with frequent and severe spontaneous panics who find them the most prominent problem, many doctors believe that medication is the most important part of treatment and reserve behavior therapy for people who avoid. Present behavioral and drug treatments for most Anxiety Disorders are effective, and individuals with these disorders have good reason to be optimistic about overcoming their problems.

Won't exposure therapy make my anxiety worse?

No. In spite of frequent and understandable worry about this possibility, exposure very seldom causes a long-term increase in anxiety. Instead, after an initial surge of anxiety, people are repeatedly surprised to find that their anxiety decreases both during an exposure session and afterwards. Only if people allow themselves to escape the feared situation soon after starting an exposure session is there a chance that they might become sensitized by the experience rather than improve.

Why will exposure work now when it hasn't all the previous times I've tried it?

It's likely that you haven't done exposure correctly in the past. In order to be helpful, exposure must be done for a long enough period of time, up to two hours or more, until anxiety has clearly decreased, and exposure should involve all the feared situations that have to be overcome. It is also important that exposure sessions occur frequently, preferably daily whenever possible. When these basic principles are put into practice systematically, either by the individual or with the help of a therapist or family member, exposure works in the great majority of cases.

What things can interfere with exposure?

Severe depression can prevent exposure from working and, if present, should be treated first. When severe depression is successfully treated, the Anxiety Disorder may also improve, especially if it began after the depression.

Alcohol or too much antianxiety medication such as benzodiazepines or barbiturates (see Chapter 7) can also impair the effectiveness of exposure treatment. They seem to disrupt the learning process.

Occasionally, family or marital problems interfere with behavior therapy. These problems are usually obvious, and this interference can often be dealt with by involving family members in the behavioral treatment, particularly in cases in which resolution of the Anxiety Disorder is likely to resolve the family or marital problem as well. In other cases, the family problems may be unrelated and may need to be solved separately from the Anxiety Disorders.

Finally, if the individual doesn't do exposure therapy properly, it will certainly not work. Just as a person with diabetes must take insulin correctly, exposure therapy cannot help an Anxiety Disorder unless it is done as prescribed.

How fast do I have to face things with exposure therapy?

The rate at which sufferers approach the things they fear is not critical. Some people prefer to proceed very gradually while others decide to push ahead rapidly. Individuals construct a hierarchy, or list of things they want to accomplish. The list goes from things that are comparatively easy to those that would be very frightening.

The amount of time people have available for treatment and any deadline by which they wish to be substantially better may determine the number of sessions and the speed with which they proceed up the hierarchy of exposure to the feared things they have been avoiding. Individuals choose how fast they will go up the hierarchy on their own or after discussing it with a therapist. In general, pick a task that you think you have a reasonable chance of accomplishing, but also one that will challenge you. A person may be able to skip some steps on the hierarchy, with the lower steps resolving automatically as the more difficult problems are tackled.

In some ways, it's like taking an adhesive bandage off of a hairy part of your body. You have the option of pulling it off slowly—one hair at a time—or yanking it off all at once.

What is the role of relaxation in treating Anxiety Disorders?
Anxiety in some people is helped, at least briefly, by training in *relaxation exercises*. Relaxation is not necessary at all to overcome phobias or obsessions, but it can help people to relieve tension temporarily. One way in which relaxation can be achieved is by developing a muscle sense through tensing one muscle group (for example, the biceps of one's arm), feeling the tension in the biceps, letting the muscle relax, and then tensing and relaxing it once more. The same is then done with other muscle groups until all of them can be easily relaxed together. These flexing and relaxing exercises can be practiced at home twice daily for 15 minutes at a time. It is usual to start with the muscles of the arms and legs and then to move to the head and neck muscles. When a patient has successfully relaxed each

important group of muscles, he or she then learns to coordinate relaxation of all these different muscle groups together. The achievement of good relaxation is indicated by stillness of the body, looseness of the muscles, regular breathing, and motionless eyelids.

When relaxing a patient, a therapist might say something along the following lines, which you could equally well say to yourself:

> Settle back as comfortably as you can. Let yourself relax to the best of your ability. . . . Now, as you relax like that, clench your right fist, just clench your fist tighter and tighter, and study the tenion as you do so. Keep it clenched and feel the tension in your right fist, hand, and forearm . . . now relax. Let the fingers of your right hand become loose and observe the contrast of feeling in your muscles. Let those muscles just relax completely. . . . Once more, clench your right fist really tight . . . hold it, and notice the tension again. . . . Now let go, relax; your fingers straighten out, and you notice the difference once more. . . . Now repeat with your left fist. Clench your left fist while the rest of your body relaxes; clench that fist tighter and feel the tension—relax and feel the difference. Continue relaxing like that for a while. . . . Clench both fists tighter and tighter, both fists tense, forearms tense, study the sensations . . . and relax: straighten out your fingers and feel that relaxation in the muscles of your hand and forearm. Continue relaxing your hands and forearms more and more. . . . Now bend your elbows and tense your biceps. . . .

Another way in which one can relax is by *autogenic training*. In this technique the person is asked to visualize one part of the body, to hold the image of that part, and then to relax it. As an example:

> Get a clear picture of your right hand, see the outline of the fingers, the color of the skin and nails, the wrinkles on your knuckles. Now relax your right hand as you think about it, keeping the image in your mind all the time. Now try to see your right forearm in your mind's eye . . . , etc.

It does not seem terribly important which mode of relaxation is used, provided the person feels completely relaxed both muscularly and mentally.

In the East various kinds of *meditation* have been developed which are also relaxing for people who practice it successfully. Some forms of meditation are said to be mastered quite quickly, for example, *mantra meditation*. In this method the subject is asked to think about a secret word and to keep that in his or her mind continually while blotting out all other thoughts, meanwhile sitting motionless. Various other methods are used in the practice of yoga and Zen meditation. Some of these approaches are said to take years to master, and people who are successful report serenity as a result. Unfortunately, we do not yet know whether very anxious people can use these techniques therapeutically.

A further method by which some people relax is by *hypnosis*. It does not matter much which method of hypnosis is used. Only a minority of people are good hypnotic subjects, although in these people hypnotic methods can be helpful to achieve relaxation. It can be very difficult to hypnotize people who are extremely anxious and who thus need relaxation most of all. While hypnosis has dramatic effects in a few people, in general hypnosis is not a reliably predictable method of overcoming fear in a lasting manner.

Methods of relaxing can help reduce free-floating anxiety for a while. However, this effect is not usually long-lasting. For the relief of phobias and obsessions that have endured for some time, exposure therapy, such as described in Chapter 10, is required.*

If I just treat the symptoms of my fear and don't get to the problem that's at its root, won't other symptoms pop up to replace the one I've gotten rid of?

The question of *symptom substitution*, as this problem is labeled, was raised by psychoanalysts and other dynamic psychotherapists many years ago as a potential drawback to behavior therapy. Several careful studies have been made of this issue, and none has found that symptom substitution occurs.

At times, though, people seeking treatment describe only some of their fears and, when those fears have been successfully treated, they reveal other fears they would like to deal with. Thus, an agoraphobic who is housebound and becomes able to travel about freely after exposure therapy may then want treatment for preexisting fears, such as fear of staying under a hair dryer or attending church, that had not been mentioned before. Success with conquering one fear breeds a desire to deal with others. You have no reason to fear that relief of your present anxiety symptoms will lead to the development of other symptoms.

When are medicines needed for panics?

When spontaneous panics are frequent and severe, then an

---

*The above information on relaxation was excerpted in revised form from *Living with Fear,* by I. M. Marks (copyright © 1978 McGraw-Hill; reprinted with permission).

antidepressant or antianxiety drug is worth trying. While many doctors would use medicines first, others prefer to begin with behavior therapy. If depression is prominent, an antidepressant is definitely indicated and, in addition to helping the depression, may also reduce the panics.

While exposure therapy avoids the side effects that can occur with medications and the high relapse rate found when medications are stopped, certain people find it difficult to carry out exposure therapy, and others may not benefit from it.

How can someone learn all that is important about anxiety and its treatment?

A book of this size cannot provide answers to every question that might be asked about anxiety. The material included here was selected because the authors—in consultation with other doctors and with actual patients—thought that it was especially important.

The following suggestions may help you learn more about anxiety and the different ways of treating it:

- Read this book and be sure to note any sections where you have questions.
- Ask your doctor these questions and any others you might have.
- Reread this book from time to time to refresh your memory. Share it with close friends and family members and discuss areas that are particularly important to you.
- Refer to the Suggested Readings on pages 240–246.

There are self-help groups around the country that offer support and information to people with Anxiety Disorders. Contact the Anxiety Disorders Center (see page 247) to find out whether there is such a program in your area. These is no charge for this information service.

When should I see a doctor or other professional about my anxiety?

Most anxiety is normal and does not need professional help. It is natural to feel worried by major examinations in school, family, illnesses, job or business pressures, or difficulties in personal relationships. Such anxiety prepares us for action so that we can cope with the problem appropriately.

An important aspect of dealing with the problem is discussing it with our friends and relatives. This can put the issues in perspective, show new angles on the problem, tell us how others coped with similar difficulties in the past, and help reduce our anxiety. In many instances, a burden shared is a burden eased. If we keep our trouble to ourselves—too ashamed to talk about it while secretly biting our nails—then we are less likely to find out all the ways there may be of coping with it. And even if the problem is inescapable, such as a fatal illness in ourselves or our loved ones, it is less difficult to bear if others share our discomfort.

Although friends, relatives, and we ourselves can be our best therapists, if the problem gets out of hand despite such common sense help, then we should seek professional help. For example, being clean and orderly may aid us in our work and is certainly something to be proud of. But if we are so consumed with worry about dirt that we spend six hours a day washing our hands until they are raw and bleeding, and if discussion with friends and relatives doesn't help, and if self-help programs like that described in Chapter 10 of this book seem too difficult, then professional help should certainly be sought. The same recommendation applies to any other sort of anxiety, whether it is fear of flying, fear of leaving home, or ongoing anxiety after experiencing a traumatic event, such as an assault. When in doubt, seek help. If you can't decide whether or not you should consult your doctor, it would be best to go ahead and do so. Even if you do not turn out to have an Anxiety Disorder, just the act of talking to your doctor can help relieve your anxiety.

But from whom should I seek help first? When should I go to a minister, social worker, psychologist, or physician?
People are most likely to go to a member of the clergy if they feel that their anxiety is "spiritual" in origin and to a doctor if it seems "medical." It is impossible to pinpoint a physical cause or drug remedy for most anxiety, and there is no hard and fast rule about whom to consult when. But if self-help and nonmedical professional aid has failed to relieve your anxiety, and if persistent life troubles are not obviously behind the worry, then you ought to see a physician to check that some medical factor has not been overlooked. When in doubt, see a doctor.

Who is the best professional to treat anxiety?
There is no simple answer to this question. Sometimes, individuals can accurately identify and treat their own problems. However, we recommend that the initial evaluation of a person with an anxiety problem be done by a professional who is experienced in diagnosing and treating anxiety problems. Many nonpsychiatric physicians are not fully aware of recent advances in the diagnosis and treatment of Anxiety Disorders. Some professionals avoid certain treatments simply because they cannot provide them. The information provided in this book should help you make an educated choice of professional. Also, there may be an Anxiety Disorders treatment center in your area or a support group that could recommend qualified therapists.

If medicine is used to treat your Anxiety Disorder, it will have to be prescribed and supervised by a medical doctor (M.D. or D.O.). If treatment involves behavior therapy, qualified therapists can include physicians, psychologists, nurses, social workers, and others. It is important to know whether an individual therapist has had special training in behavioral techniques; this may be as important as the actual degree held by a therapist.

Are there specialists who treat Anxiety Disorders?

Yes. While many Anxiety Disorders can be effectively treated by primary care physicians, general psychiatrists, psychologists, and by patients themselves, some require a more specialized approach. There are individuals and groups who deal with Anxiety Disorders as a specialty area. For example, the Anxiety Disorders Center at the University of Wisconsin specializes in the evaluation and treatment of these disorders, provides information to professionals and the general public, conducts educational programs, provides speakers, and does research on Anxiety Disorders. The Anxiety Disorders Center attempts to keep a list of reputable anxiety therapists in different geographic areas and provides this information without charge (see page 247 for the address).

12
Summing Up

ANXIETY may be helpful or harmful. When anxiety stimulates us to prepare and helps us to perform it is helpful. If anxiety is so severe and persistent that it interferes with our functioning and causes suffering, either because of the anxiety itself or because of the effects of anxiety on our functioning, it is harmful. Even at its worst, anxiety is probably not a significant hazard to our physical health or longevity—but it can certainly be unpleasant. When anxiety reaches disturbing proportions either in terms of duration or severity, help is available.

The Anxiety Disorders are grouped together because anxiety is the major symptom of each of them. The prominence of anxiety sets them apart from depression or schizophrenia, in which some anxiety may be present but is far less prominent than problems of depressed mood or abnormal thinking (such as delusions and hallucinations). Even though

Anxiety Disorders have marked anxiety as a common feature, they differ from one another in many important ways. Some of the phobias of childhood are so common and stop so predictably without treatment that they are seldom considered disorders. Other phobias (including Agoraphobia and Social Phobia) and Obsessive-Compulsive Disorder may substantially interfere with functioning and last for years or even decades if untreated. Chronic Post-Traumatic Stress Disorder may also last for many years, is difficult to treat, and may cause severe handicap. The frequency, severity, and type of anxiety differ substantially across the several Anxiety Disorders. At one extreme, people with an Anxiety Disorder experience mild but rather constant anxiety, while at the other extreme they have infrequent, brief, but terrifying panic. Anxiety may occur only in specific situations or regardless of where the person is.

The differences among Anxiety Disorders are important because they provide clues to the likely course of the disorder and guidance in selecting the best treatment for each disorder.

While some Anxiety Disorders are easily recognized by patients and family members, most of the time it is wise to see a doctor who is experienced with Anxiety Disorders for evaluation and diagnosis.

Behavior therapy is the treatment of choice for Phobic Disorders and Obsessive-Compulsive Disorders. Panic brought on by specific objects or situations, anxiety about encountering objects or entering situations, and avoidance of objects and situations all respond to behavior therapy. Frequent and prolonged exposure to the things people fear produces a gratifying decrease in anxiety in almost all patients. The techniques of effective behavior therapy are straightforward and simple to learn, and many patients will be able to use the techniques of behavior therapy outlined in Chapter 10 on their own. Family members can often play a useful role in treating Anxiety Disorders once they learn the techniques of exposure and response prevention. Improvements obtained with behavior therapy are substantial and long-lasting. At times, help from a doctor may be needed to refine the use of behavioral treatments.

Medications are also important in the treatment of certain Anxiety Disorders. Many doctors feel they are the treatment of choice for Panic Disorder when panic arises spontaneously— "out of the blue"—without any identifiable cause. Unfortunately, relapse after discontinuing medication is the rule rather than the exception, but there is no doubt that antidepressant and antianxiety medications, when properly prescribed, can often block or reduce spontaneous panic. Medications may also be used as adjunctive treatments in Phobic and Obsessive-Compulsive Disorders, although their use in these disorders remains somewhat controversial. Many people receive antianxiety drugs for brief periods of situational anxiety that are unusual for them. Relief of these anxiety states is often substantial, and functioning is improved until they have time to recover from whatever stressful situations are bothering them. Support and reassurance are also important at times of distress and should not be overlooked. Obviously, patients being treated with medications must be under the care of a physician who can prescribe and monitor them.

We recommend that Phobic and Obsessive-Compulsive Disorders first be treated with behavioral treatments, which are most likely to be helpful, have fewer and less troubling side effects, and have lower relapse rates than medications. We recognize, however, that other competent physicians will prefer medication or psychotherapy as primary treatments, and some may feel that they would like to provide behavior therapy but do not have the time (or training) to do so. We also recognize that some patients may not have the time or inclination to participate in behavior therapy yet may benefit from an alternative treatment.

In the end, it is often necessary to carefully tailor treatments to each person's problems, beliefs, resources, and experience. As one patient wrote after attending a professional conference on Anxiety Disorders,

> I certainly enjoyed hearing "both sides of the story," but I couldn't help thinking that I'd probably have dropped out of both "Doctor Behavior Therapy's" and "Doctor Drug Therapy's" programs. Thanks to the fine blend of both that you used, I'm happy and grateful to be listed among the treatment successes and not the failures.

We hope that this book is helpful to patients receiving behavior therapy, medications, psychotherapy, or a combination of these treatments. Some people will be able to recognize their disorders and relieve them effectively on their own. Others will need full evaluations and ongoing treatment by a doctor. We hope that all people with anxiety and Anxiety Disorders will be able to find descriptions in this book that are consistent with their own experience, and that they will learn enough about the treatments of their disorders to know that HELP IS AVAILABLE.

Suggested Readings

The following books may be helpful in better understanding anxiety, anxiety disorders, and depression, which often accompanies and sometimes causes anxiety disorders. (Prices listed are accurate as of January 1986.)

NONTECHNICAL BOOKS

Advice for the Patient, Sixth Edition (Volume II of *USP-Dispensing Information*), by the United States Pharmacopeial Convention, Inc., 12601 Twinbrook Parkway, Rockville, MD 20852. 1986. 1162 p. $23.95

Agoraphobia: Nature and Treatment, by A. M. Mathew, M. G. Gelder, and D. W. Johnston. Guilford Press, New York, 1981. 233 p. $25.00

A comprehensive discussion of agoraphobia. Includes treatment manuals for the patient and a partner (cotherapist) that have been tried, tested, and found helpful in a controlled trial.

Anxiety, by D. W. Goodwin. Oxford University Press, New York, 1986. 234 p. $17.95

Entertaining history of anxiety disorders, their diagnosis, and treatment.

Depression and Its Treatment: Help for the Nation's #1 Mental Problem, by J. H. Greist and J. W. Jefferson. Quality paperback edition: American Psychiatric Press, Inc., Washington, D.C., 1984. 128 p. $7.95; Mass market paperback edition: Warner Books, 1985. 118 p., $3.95

Describes depression in its various forms and the ways in which depression is treated.

Freedom from Compulsion, by L. Cammer. Simon and Schuster, New York, 1976. 271 p. Out of Print (may be available in libraries)

Good descriptions of obsessive-compulsive phenomena.

Living with Fear, by I. M. Marks. McGraw-Hill, New York, 1980. 320 p. Paperback, $6.95

Comprehensive presentation of anxiety and anxiety disorders including sexual anxieties. Chapter 10 from the book you are now reading first appeared in *Living with Fear.* It is one of the few self-help manuals to be tried, tested, and found helpful in a controlled study.

Mind, Mood, and Medicine: A Guide to the New Biopsychiatry, by P. H. Wender and D. F. Klein. Hardbound edition: Farrar, Straus & Giroux, New York, 1981, 372 p. $16.95; Paperback edition: New American Library, New York, 1982, $7.95

A well written discussion of the biological approach to psychiatric disorders.

National Phobia Treatment Directory (Second Edition), by the Phobia Society of America, 5820 Hubbard Drive, Rockville, Maryland 20852. 1986. 65 p. $5.50

Lists therapists who reputedly have training and skill in treating phobias.

Panic: Facing Fears, Phobias, and Anxiety, by W. S. Agras. W. H. Freeman, New York, 1985. 151 p. $11.95

An excellent review of anxiety disorders and their treatments.

Phobia (Facts Series), by Donald W. Goodwin. Oxford University Press, New York, 1983. 149 p. $13.95

Charming descriptions of phobias and their treatments.

The Anxiety Disease and How to Overcome It, by D. V. Sheehan. Scribners, New York, 1984. 224 p. $14.95

Presents arguments for panic disorder being a biological disorder.

Your Phobia: Understanding Your Fears Through Contextual Therapy, by M. D. Zane and H. Milt. American Psychiatric Press, Inc., Washington, D.C., 1984. 280 p. $15.95

An approach to treatment of phobias that has helped many patients with phobias.

RUNNING GUIDES

Running Guides, by R. R. Eischens and J. H. Greist. Anxiety Disorders Center, 600 Highland Avenue, Madison, Wisconsin 53792. 1980. 102 p. $3.00

Two guides for individuals about to begin a walking-jogging-running program for physical and emotional well being.

TECHNICAL BOOKS

Anxiety and the Anxiety Disorders, edited by H. A. Tuma and J. D. Maser. Lawrence Erlbaum, Inc., Hillsdale, NJ, 1985. 1020 p. $95.00

A comprehensive account of anxiety disorders and their treatment in 42 chapters by 60 authors.

Anxiety and Emotions: Physiological Basis and Treatment, by D. Kelly. Charles C. Thomas, Springfield, Illinois, 1980. 424 p. $24.75

An account of the physiology and neurophysiology of anxiety. Especially detailed account of the effects of psychosurgery.

Anxiety Disorders and Phobias: A Cognitive Perspective, by A. T. Beck and G. Emery. Basic Books, New York, 1985. 416 p. $26.95

The theory and technique of cognitive behavior therapy for anxiety disorders is presented.

Anxiety: New Research and Changing Concepts, edited by D. F. Klein and J. G. Rabkin. Raven Press, New York, 1981. 454 p. Out of Print (may be available in medical libraries)

Twenty-eight chapters by 73 authors and coauthors review findings from the areas of psychopharmacology, neuroendocrinology, genetics, and behavioral treatment and analyze their implications in terms of major theories of the psychopathology of anxiety disorders.

Biology of Agoraphobia, edited by J. C. Ballenger. American Psychiatric Press, Inc., Washington, D.C., 1984. 128 p. $12.00

Twenty-two authors wrote five chapters on biological aspects of agoraphobia.

Diagnosis and Treatment of Anxiety Disorder, edited by R. O. Pasnau. American Psychiatric Press, Inc., Washington, D.C., 1984. 272 p. $26.00

Ten authors describe various aspects of anxiety disorders and the treatment on panic, anxiety, and its disorders.

Fears, Phobias, and Rituals: An Interdisciplinary Perspective, by I. M. Marks. Oxford University Press, New York, 1986. 700 p. Price not announced.

Sixteen chapters by one author reviewing normal and abnormal fears and rituals from the points of view of ethology, development, genetics, physiology, learning, clinical picture, and behavioral and drug treatments with an up-to-date review of findings (contains about 3,000 references).

New Findings in Obsessive-Compulsive Disorder, edited by T. R. Insel. American Psychiatric Press, Inc., Washington, D.C., 1984. 136 p. Paperback, $12.00

Nine contributors present six chapters on clinical presentation and different treatments of obsessive-compulsive disorder.

Obsessions and Compulsions, by S. J. Rachman and R. J. Hodgson. Prentice-Hall, Inc., Englewood Cliffs, New Jersey, 1980. 437 p. $35.95

A comprehensive treatment of obsessive-compulsive disorder with detailed discussions of the limitations of the various treatment approaches.

Phobia: Psychological and Pharmacological Treatment, edited by M. Mavissakalian and D. H. Barlow. Guilford Press, New York, 1981. 256 p. $20.00

Nine contributors present their views on changes in behavioral and drug treatments of anxiety disorders.

Treatment of Mental Disorders, edited by J. H. Greist, J. W. Jefferson, and R. L. Spitzer. Oxford University Press, New York, 1982. 548 p. Paperback, $24.95

Nineteen chapters by 27 authors and coauthors cover treatments of psychiatric disorders of adults, sleep disorders, and treatment compliance.

Feedback Form

ALTHOUGH the treatments described in this book have helped many sufferers, they don't work for everybody. The authors are always looking for ways to refine their methods. If you wish to aid this ongoing process by writing of your experiences, photocopy the form on these two pages and mail it to them in care of:

Dr. Greist
Anxiety Disorders Center
University of Wisconsin Hospital
600 Highland Avenue
Madison, Wisconsin 53792-9968

1. What I liked about your book or treatment methods:___

_____

_____

2. What I didn't like about your book or treatment methods:_____

_____

_____

3. Your treatment suggestions that I personally found most helpful:_____

_____

_____

4. Changes I think you might make in the light of my personal experience:_____

_____

_____

5. Other comments:_____

_____

_____

Name (optional): _____

Address (optional): _____

Appendix

The material in this Appendix has been excerpted from the *Diagnostic and Statistical Manual of Mental Disorders*, Third Edition (DSM-III), published in 1980 by the American Psychiatric Association, 1400 K Street, N.W., Washington, DC 20005. Reprinted by permission.

Anxiety Disorders

In this group of disorders anxiety is either the predominant disturbance, as in Panic Disorder and Generalized Anxiety Disorder, or anxiety is experienced if the individual attempts to master the symptoms, as in confronting the dreaded object or situation in a Phobic Disorder or resisting the obsessions or compulsions in Obsessive Compulsive Disorder. Diagnosis of an Anxiety Disorder is not made if the anxiety is due to another disorder, such as Schizophrenia, an Affective Disorder, or an Organic Mental Disorder.

It has been estimated that from 2% to 4% of the general population has at some time had a disorder that this manual would classify as an Anxiety Disorder.

Panic Disorder, Phobic Disorders and Obsessive Compulsive Disorder are each apparently more common among family members of individuals with each of these disorders than in the general population.

PHOBIC DISORDERS (OR PHOBIC NEUROSES)

The essential feature is persistent and irrational fear of a specific object, activity, or situation that results in a compelling desire to avoid the dreaded object, activity, or situation (the phobic stimulus). The fear is recognized by the individual as excessive or unreasonable in proportion to the actual dangerousness of the object, activity, or situation.

Irrational avoidance of objects, activities, or situations that has an insignificant effect on life adjustment is commonplace. For example, many individuals experience some irrational fear when unable to avoid contact with harmless insects or spiders, but this has no major effect on their lives. However, when the avoidance behavior or fear is a significant source of distress to the individual or interferes with social or role functioning, a diagnosis of a Phobic Disorder is warranted.

The Phobic Disorders are subdivided into three types: Agoraphobia, the most severe and pervasive form; Social Phobia; and Simple Phobia. Both Social and Simple Phobias generally involve a circumscribed stimulus, but Simple Phobia tends to have an earlier onset and better prognosis. When more than one type is present, multiple diagnoses should be made.

Although anxiety related to separation from parental figures is a form of phobic reaction, it is classified as Separation Anxiety Disorder, in the section Disorders Usually First Evident in Infancy, Childhood, or Adolescence (p. 50). Similarly, phobic avoidance limited to sexual activities is classified as a Psychosexual Disorder Not Elsewhere Classified (p. 282).

Although Simple Phobia is the most common type of Phobic Disorder in the general population, Agoraphobia is the most common among those seeking treatment.

300.21 Agoraphobia with Panic Attacks

300.22 Agoraphobia without Panic Attacks

The essential feature is a marked fear of being alone, or being in public places from which escape might be difficult or help not available in case of sudden incapacitation. Normal activities are increasingly constricted as the fears or avoidance behavior dominate the individual's life. The most common situations avoided involve being in crowds, such as on a busy street or in crowded stores, or being in tunnels, on bridges, on elevators, or on public transportation. Often these individuals insist that a family member or friend accompany them whenever they leave home.

The disturbance is not due to a major depressive episode, Obsessive Compulsive Disorder, Paranoid Personality Disorder, or Schizophrenia.

Often the initial phase of the disorder consists of recurrent panic attacks. (For a description of panic attacks, see p. 230.) The individual develops anticipatory fear of having such an attack and becomes reluctant or refuses to enter a variety of situations that are associated with these attacks. When there is a history of panic attacks (which may or may not be currently present) associated with avoidance behavior, the diagnosis of Agoraphobia with Panic Attacks should be made. Where there is no such history (or this information is lacking), the diagnosis of Agoraphobia without Panic Attacks should be made.

Associated features. Depression, anxiety, rituals, minor "checking" compulsions, or rumination is frequently present.

Age at onset. Most frequently the onset is in the late teens or early 20s, but it can be much later.

Course. The severity of the disturbance waxes and wanes, and periods of complete remission are possible. The activities or situations that the individual dreads may change from day to day.

Impairment. During exacerbations of the illness the individual may be housebound. The avoidance of certain situations, such as being in elevators, may grossly interfere with social and occupational functioning.

Complications. Some individuals attempt to relieve their anxiety with alcohol, barbiturates, or antianxiety medications even to the extent of becoming physiologically dependent on them. Major Depression is another complication.

Predisposing factors. Separation Anxiety Disorder in childhood and sudden object less apparently predispose to the development of Agoraphobia.

Prevalence. A study of the general population in a small city found that approximately 0.5% of the population had had Agoraphobia at some time.

Sex ratio. The disorder is more frequently diagnosed in women.

Differential diagnosis. In **Schizophrenia, Major Depression, Obsessive Compulsive Disorder** and **Paranoid Personality Disorder** there may be phobic avoidance of certain situations. The diagnosis of Agoraphobia is not made if a phobia is due to any of these disorders.

Diagnostic criteria for Agoraphobia

A. The individual has marked fear of and thus avoids being alone or in public places from which escape might be difficult or help not available in case of sudden incapacitation, e.g., crowds, tunnels, bridges, public transportation.

B. There is increasing constriction of normal activities until the fears or avoidance behavior dominate the individual's life.

C. Not due to a major depressive episode, Obsessive Compulsive Disorder, Paranoid Personality Disorder, or Schizophrenia.

300.23 Social Phobia

The essential feature is a persistent, irrational fear of, and compelling desire to avoid, situations in which the individual may be exposed to scrutiny by others. There is also fear that the individual may behave in a manner that will be humiliating or embarrassing. Marked anticipatory anxiety occurs if the individual is confronted with the necessity of entering into such a situation, and he or she therefore attempts to avoid it. The disturbance is a significant source of distress and is recognized by the individual as excessive or unreasonable. It is not due to any other mental disorder. Examples of Social Phobias are fears of speaking or performing in public, using public lavatories, eating in public, and writing in the presence of others. Generally an individual has only one Social Phobia.

Usually the individual is aware that the fear is that others will detect signs of anxiety in the phobic situation. For example, the individual with a fear of writing in the presence of others is concerned that others may detect a hand tremor. A vicious cycle may be created in which the irrational fear generates anxiety that impairs performance, thus providing an apparent justification for avoiding the phobic situation.

Associated features. Considerable unfocused or generalized anxiety may also be present. Agoraphobia or Simple Phobia may coexist with Social Phobia.

Age at onset. The disorder often begins in late childhood or early adolescence.

Course. The disorder is usually chronic, and may undergo exacerbation when the anxiety impairs performance of the feared activity. This then leads to increased anxiety, which strengthens the phobic avoidance.

Impairment. Unless the disorder is severe, it is rarely, in itself, incapacitating. However, considerable inconvenience may result from the need to avoid the phobic situation, e.g., avoiding a trip if it would necessitate the use of a public lavatory. Fear of public speaking may interfere with professional advancement.

Complications. Individuals with this disorder are prone to the episodic abuse of alcohol, barbiturates, and antianxiety medications, which they may use to relieve their anxiety.

Prevalence. The disorder is apparently relatively rare.

Predisposing factors, sex ratio, and familial pattern. No information.

Differential diagnosis. Avoidance of certain social situations that are normally a source of some distress, which is common in many individuals with "normal" fear of public speaking, does not justify a diagnosis of Social Phobia. In **Schizophrenia, Major Depression, Obsessive Compulsive Disorder,** and **Paranoid** and **Avoidant Personality Disorders,** there may be marked anxiety and avoidance of certain social situations. However, the diagnosis of Social Phobia is not made if the phobia is due to any of these disorders.

In **Simple Phobia** there is also a circumscribed phobic stimulus, but it is not a social situation involving the possibility of humiliation or embarrassment.

Diagnostic criteria for Social Phobia
A. A persistent, irrational fear of, and compelling desire to avoid, a situation in which the individual is exposed to possible scrutiny by

others and fears that he or she may act in a way
that will be humiliating or embarrassing.

B. Significant distress because of the disturbance
and recognition by the individual that his or her
fear is excessive or unreasonable.

C. Not due to another mental disorder, such as
Major Depression or Avoidant Personality Disorder.

300.29 Simple Phobia

The essential feature is a persistent, irrational fear of,
and compelling desire to avoid, an object or a situation other than being alone or in public places away
from home (Agoraphobia), or of humiliation or embarrassment in certain social situations (Social Phobia). Thus, this is a residual category of Phobic Disorder. This disturbance is a significant source of distress,
and the individual recognizes that his or her fear is
excessive or unreasonable. The disturbance is not due
to another mental disorder.

Simple Phobias are sometimes referred to as "specific" phobias. The most common Simple Phobias in
the general population, though not necessarily among
those seeking treatment, involve animals, particularly
dogs, snakes, insects, and mice. Other Simple Phobias
are claustrophobia (fear of close spaces) and acropho-
bia (fear of heights).

Associated features. When suddenly exposed to
the phobic stimulus, the individual becomes over-
whelmingly fearful and may experience symptoms
identical with those of a panic attack (p. 230). Be-

cause of anticipatory anxiety, the individual will often try to gain considerable information before entering situations in which the phobic stimulus may be encountered.

Age at onset. Age at onset varies, but animal phobias nearly always begin in childhood.

Course. Most simple phobias that start in childhood disappear without treatment. However, those that persist into adulthood rarely remit without treatment.

Impairment. Impairment may be minimal if the phobic object is rare and easily avoided, such as fear of snakes in someone living in the city. Impairment may be considerable if the phobic object is common and cannot be avoided, such as a fear of elevators in someone living in a large city who must use elevators at work.

Complications and predisposing factors. No information.

Prevalence. Simple Phobias may be common; but since they rarely result in marked impairment, individuals with Simple Phobia rarely seek treatment.

Sex ratio. The disorder is more often diagnosed in women.

Differential diagnosis. In **Schizophrenia** certain activities may be avoided in response to delusions. Similarly, in **Obsessive Compulsive Disorder** phobic avoidance of certain situations that are associated with anxiety about dirt or contamination is frequent. The diagnosis of Simple Phobia should not be made in either case.

> ### Diagnostic criteria for Simple Phobia
> A. A persistent, irrational fear of, and compelling desire to avoid, an object or a situation other than being alone, or in public places away from home (Agoraphobia), or of humiliation or embarrassment in certain social situations (Social Phobia). Phobic objects are often animals, and phobic situations frequently involve heights or closed spaces.
>
> B. Significant distress from the disturbance and recognition by the individual that his or her fear is excessive or unreasonable.
>
> C. Not due to another mental disorder, such as Schizophrenia or Obsessive Compulsive Disorder.

ANXIETY STATES (OR ANXIETY NEUROSES)

300.01 Panic Disorder

The essential features are recurrent panic (anxiety) attacks that occur at times unpredictably, though certain situations, e.g., driving a car, may become associated with a panic attack. The same clinical picture occurring during marked physical exertion or a life-threatening situation is not termed a panic attack.

The panic attacks are manifested by the sudden onset of intense apprehension, fear, or terror, often associated with feelings of impending doom. The most common symptoms experienced during an attack are dyspnea; palpitations; chest pain or discomfort; choking or smothering sensations; dizziness, vertigo, or unsteady feelings; feelings of unreality (depersonalization or derealization); paresthesias; hot and cold flashes; sweating; faintness; trembling or shaking; and fear of dying, going crazy, or doing something uncontrolled during the attack. Attacks usually last minutes; more rarely, hours.

A common complication of this disorder is the development of an anticipatory fear of helplessness or loss of control during a panic attack, so that the individual becomes reluctant to be alone or in public places away from home. When many situations of the kind are avoided the diagnosis of Agoraphobia with Panic Attacks should be made (p. 226) rather than Panic Disorder.

Associated features. The individual often develops varying degrees of nervousness and apprehension between attacks. This nervousness and apprehension is characterized by the usual manifestations of apprehensive expectation, vigilance and scanning, motor tension, and autonomic hyperactivity.

Age at onset. The disorder often begins in late adolescence or early adult life, but may occur initially in mid-adult life.

Course. The disorder may be limited to a single brief period lasting several weeks or months, recur several times, or become chronic.

Impairment. Except when the disorder is severe or complicated by Agoraphobia, it is rarely incapacitating.

Complications. The complication of Agoraphobia with Panic Attacks has been mentioned above. Other complications include abuse of alcohol and antianxiety medications, and Depressive Disorders.

Predisposing factors. Separation Anxiety Disorder in childhood and sudden object loss apparently predispose to the development of this disorder.

Prevalence. The disorder is apparently common.

Sex ratio. This condition is diagnosed much more commonly in women.

Differential diagnosis. Physical disorders such as **hypoglycemia, pheochromocytoma,** and **hyperthyroidism,** all of which can cause similar symptoms, must be ruled out.

In **Withdrawal** from some substances, such as **barbiturates,** and in some **Substance Intoxications,** such as due to **caffeine** or **amphetamines,** there may be panic attacks. Panic Disorder should not be diagnosed when the panic attacks are due to Substance-induced Organic Mental Disorder.

In **Schizophrenia, Major Depression,** or **Somatization Disorder** panic attacks may occur. However, the diagnosis of Panic Disorder is not made if the panic attacks are due to these other disorders.

Generalized Anxiety Disorder may be confused with the chronic anxiety that often develops between panic attacks in Panic Disorder. A history of recurrent panic attacks precludes Generalized Anxiety Disorder.

In **Simple** or **Social Phobia,** the individual may develop panic attacks if exposed to the phobic stimulus. However, in Panic Disorder, the individual is never certain which situations provoke panic attacks.

Diagnostic criteria for Panic Disorder

A. At least three panic attacks within a three-week period in circumstances other than during marked physical exertion or in a life-threatening situation. The attacks are not precipitated only by exposure to a circumscribed phobic stimulus.

B. Panic attacks are manifested by discrete periods of apprehension or fear, and at least four of the following symptoms appear during each attack:

   (1) dyspnea
   (2) palpitations
   (3) chest pain or discomfort
   (4) choking or smothering sensations
   (5) dizziness, vertigo, or unsteady feelings
   (6) feelings of unreality
   (7) paresthesias (tingling in hands or feet)
   (8) hot and cold flashes
   (9) sweating
  (10) faintness
  (11) trembling or shaking
  (12) fear of dying, going crazy, or doing something uncontrolled during an attack

C. Not due to a physical disorder or another mental disorder, such as Major Depression, Somatization Disorder, or Schizophrenia.

D. The disorder is not associated with Agoraphobia (p. 227).

300.02 Generalized Anxiety Disorder

The essential feature is generalized, persistent anxiety of at least one month's duration without the specific symptoms that characterize Phobic Disorders (phobias), Panic Disorder (panic attacks), or Obsessive Compulsive Disorder (obsessions or compulsions). The diagnosis is not made if the disturbance is due to another physical or mental disorder, such as hyperthyroidism or Major Depression.

Although the specific manifestations of the anxiety vary from individual to individual, generally there are signs of motor tension, autonomic hyperactivity, apprehensive expectation, and vigilance and scanning.

(1) *Motor tension.* Shakiness, jitteriness, jumpiness, trembling, tension, muscle aches, fatigability, and inability to relax are common complaints. There may also be eyelid twitch, furrowed brow, strained face, fidgeting, restlessness, easy startle, and sighing respiration.

(2) *Autonomic hyperactivity.* There may be sweating, heart pounding or racing, cold, clammy hands, dry mouth, dizziness, light-headedness, paresthesias (tingling in hands or feet), upset stomach, hot or cold spells, frequent urination, diarrhea, discomfort in the pit of the stomach, lump in the throat, flushing, pallor, and high resting pulse and respiration rate.

(3) *Apprehensive expectation.* The individual is generally apprehensive and continually feels anxious, worries, ruminates, and anticipates that something bad will happen to himself or herself (e.g., fear of fainting,

losing control, dying) or to others (e.g., family members may become ill or injured in an accident).

(4) Vigilance and scanning. Apprehensive expectation may cause hyperattentiveness so that the individual feels "on edge," impatient, or irritable. There may be complaints of distractibility, difficulty in concentrating, insomnia, difficulty in falling asleep, interrupted sleep, and fatigue on awakening.

Associated features. Mild depressive symptoms are common.

Impairment. Impairment in social or occupational functioning is rarely more than mild.

Complications. Abuse of alcohol, barbiturates, and antianxiety medications is common.

Age at onset, course, predisposing factors, prevalence, sex ratio, and familial pattern. No information.

Differential diagnosis. Physical disorders, such as hyperthyroidism, and Organic Mental Disorders, such as Caffeine Intoxication, must be ruled out.

In **Adjustment Disorder with Anxious Mood,** the full symptom picture required to meet the criteria for Generalized Anxiety Disorder is generally not present, the duration of the disturbance is usually less than a month, and a psychosocial stressor must be recognized.

In **Schizophrenia, Depressive Disorders, Hypochondriasis, Obsessive Compulsive Disorder,** and many other mental disorders, generalized and persistent anxiety is often a prominent symptom. The diagnosis of Generalized Anxiety Disorder is not made if the anxiety is judged to be due to another mental disorder.

In **Panic Disorder** there is often severe chronic anxiety between panic attacks. If the panic attacks are overlooked, an incorrect diagnosis of Generalized Anxiety Disorder may be made.

Diagnostic criteria for Generalized Anxiety Disorder

A. Generalized, persistent anxiety is manifested by symptoms from three of the following four categories:

(1) motor tension: shakiness, jitteriness, jumpiness, trembling, tension, muscle aches, fatigability, inability to relax, eyelid twitch, furrowed brow, strained face, fidgeting, restlessness, easy startle

(2) autonomic hyperactivity: sweating, heart pounding or racing, cold, clammy hands, dry mouth, dizziness, light-headedness, paresthesias (tingling in hands or feet), upset stomach, hot or cold spells, frequent urination, diarrhea, discomfort in the pit of the stomach, lump in the throat, flushing, pallor, high resting pulse and respiration rate

(3) apprehensive expectation: anxiety, worry, fear, rumination, and anticipation of misfortune to self or others

(4) vigilance and scanning: hyperattentiveness resulting in distractibility, difficulty in concentrating, insomnia, feeling "on edge," irritability, impatience

B. The anxious mood has been continuous for at least one month.

C. Not due to another mental disorder, such as a Depressive Disorder or Schizophrenia.

D. At least 18 years of age.

300.30 Obsessive Compulsive Disorder (or Obsessive Compulsive Neurosis)

The essential features are recurrent obsessions or compulsions. *Obsessions* are recurrent, persistent ideas, thoughts, images, or impulses that are ego-dystonic, that is, they are not experienced as voluntarily produced, but rather as thoughts that invade consciousness and are experienced as senseless or repugnant. Attempts are made to ignore or suppress them. *Compulsions* are repetitive and seemingly purposeful behaviors that are performed according to certain rules or in a stereotyped fashion. The behavior is not an end in itself, but is designed to produce or to prevent some future event or situation. However, the activity is not connected in a realistic way with what it is designed to produce or prevent, or may be clearly excessive. The act is performed with a sense of subjective compulsion coupled with a desire to resist the compulsion (at least initially). The individual generally recognizes the senselessness of the behavior (this may not be true for young children) and does not derive pleasure from carrying out the activity, although it provides a release of tension.

The most common obsessions are repetitive thoughts of violence (e.g., killing one's child), contamination (e.g., becoming infected by shaking hands), and doubt (e.g., repeatedly wondering whether one has performed some action, such as having hurt someone in a traffic accident). The most common compulsions involve hand-washing, counting, checking, and touching.

When the individual attempts to resist a compulsion, there is a sense of mounting tension that can be immediately relieved by yielding to the compulsion. In the course of the illness, after repeated failure at resisting the compulsions, the individual may give in to them and no longer experience a desire to resist them.

Associated features. Depression and anxiety are common. Frequently there is phobic avoidance of situations that involve the content of the obsessions, such as dirt or contamination.

Age at onset. Although the disorder usually begins in adolescence or early adulthood, it may begin in childhood.

Course. The course is usually chronic, with waxing and waning of symptoms.

Impairment. Impairment is generally moderate to severe. In some cases compulsions may become the major life activity.

Complications. Complications include Major Depression and the abuse of alcohol and antianxiety medications.

Predisposing factors. No information.

Prevalence. The disorder is apparently rare in the general population.

Sex ratio. This disorder is equally common in males and in females.

Differential diagnosis. Some activities, such as **eating, sexual behavior (e.g., Paraphilias), gambling, or drinking, when engaged in excessively** may be referred to as "compulsive." However, these activities are not true compulsions, because the individual derives pleasure from the particular activity and may wish to resist it only because of its secondary deleterious consequences.

Obsessive brooding, rumination or **preoccupation,** i.e., excessive and repetitive thinking about real or potentially unpleasant circumstances, or indecisive consideration of alternatives lacks the quality of being ego-dystonic, because the individual generally regards the ideation as meaningful, although possibly excessive. Therefore, these are not true obsessions.

In **Schizophrenia,** stereotyped behavior is common, but can be explained by delusions rather than as being ego-dystonic. Obsessions and compulsions sometimes occur transiently during the prodromal phase of Schizophrenia. In such cases the diagnosis of Obsessive Compulsive Disorder is not made. **Tourette's Disorder, Schizophrenia, Major Depression** and, very rarely, **Organic Mental Disorder** may have obsessions and compulsions as symptoms, but in such instances the diagnosis Obsessive Compulsive Disorder is not made. However, Obsessive Compulsive Disorder may precede the development of a Major Depression, in which case both diagnoses should be recorded.

Diagnostic criteria for Obsessive Compulsive Disorder

A. Either obsessions or compulsions:

Obsessions: recurrent, persistent ideas, thoughts, images, or impulses that are ego-dystonic, i.e., they are not experienced as voluntarily produced, but rather as thoughts that invade consciousness and are experienced as senseless or repugnant. Attempts are made to ignore or suppress them.

Compulsions: repetitive and seemingly purposeful behaviors that are performed according to certain rules or in a stereotyped fashion. The behavior is not an end in itself, but is designed to produce or prevent some future event or situation. However, either the activity is not connected in a realistic way with what it is designed to produce or prevent, or may be clearly excessive. The act is performed with a sense of subjective compulsion coupled with a desire to resist the compulsion (at least initially). The individual generally recognizes the senselessness of the behavior (this may not be true for young children) and does not derive pleasure from carrying out the activity, although it provides a release of tension.

B. The obsessions or compulsions are a significant source of distress to the individual or interfere with social or role functioning.

C. Not due to another mental disorder, such as Tourette's Disorder, Schizophrenia, Major Depression, or Organic Mental Disorder.

308.30 Post-traumatic Stress Disorder, Acute

309.81 Post-traumatic Stress Disorder, Chronic or Delayed

The essential feature is the development of characteristic symptoms following a psychologically traumatic event that is generally outside the range of usual human experience.

The characteristic symptoms involve reexperiencing the traumatic event; numbing of responsiveness to, or reduced involvement with, the external world; and a variety of autonomic, dysphoric, or cognitive symptoms.

The stressor producing this syndrome would evoke significant symptoms of distress in most people, and is generally outside the range of such common experiences as simple bereavement, chronic illness, business losses, or marital conflict. The trauma may be experienced alone (rape or assault) or in the company of groups of people (military combat). Stressors producing this disorder include natural disasters (floods, earthquakes), accidental man-made disasters (car accidents with serious physical injury, airplane crashes, large fires), or deliberate man-made disasters (bombing, torture, death camps). Some stressors frequently produce the disorder (e.g., torture) and others produce it only occasionally (e.g., car accidents). Frequently there is a concomitant physical component to the trauma which may even involve direct damage to the central nervous system (e.g., malnutrition, head trauma). The disorder is apparently more severe and longer lasting when the stressor is of human design. The severity of the stressor should be recorded and the specific stressor may be noted on Axis IV (p. 26).

The traumatic event can be reexperienced in a variety of ways. Commonly the individual has recurrent painful, intrusive recollections of the event or recurrent dreams or nightmares during which the event is reexperienced. In rare instances there are dissociative-like states, lasting from a few minutes to several hours or even days, during which components of the event are relived and the individual behaves as though experiencing the event at that moment. Such states have been reported in combat veterans. Diminished responsiveness to the external world, referred to as "psychic numbing" or "emotional anesthesia," usually begins soon after the traumatic event. A person may complain of feeling detached or estranged from other people, that he or she has lost the ability to become interested in previously enjoyed significant activities, or that the ability to feel emotions of any type, especially those associated with intimacy, tenderness, and sexuality, is markedly decreased.

After experiencing the stressor, many develop symptoms of excessive autonomic arousal, such as hyperalertness, exaggerated startle response, and difficulty falling asleep. Recurrent nightmares during which the traumatic event is relived and which are sometimes accompanied by middle or terminal sleep disturbance may be present. Some complain of impaired memory or difficulty in concentrating or completing tasks. In the case of a life-threatening trauma shared with others, survivors often describe painful guilt feelings about surviving when many did not, or about the things they had to do in order to survive. Activities or situations that may arouse recollections of the traumatic event are often avoided. Symptoms characteristic of Post-traumatic Stress Disorder are often intensified when the individual is exposed to situations or activities that resemble or symbolize the original trauma (e.g., cold snowy weather or uniformed guards for death-camp survivors, hot, humid weather for veterans of the South Pacific).

Associated features. Symptoms of depression and anxiety are common, and in some instances may be sufficiently severe to be diagnosed as an Anxiety or Depressive Disorder. Increased irritability may be associated with sporadic and unpredictable explosions of aggressive behavior, upon even minimal or no provocation. The latter symptom has been reported to be particularly characteristic of war veterans with this disorder. Impulsive behavior can occur, such as sudden trips, unexplained absences, or changes in lifestyle or residence. Survivors of death camps sometimes have symptoms of an Organic Mental Disorder, such as failing memory, difficulty in concentrating, emotional lability, autonomic lability, headache, and vertigo.

Age at onset. The disorder can occur at any age, including during childhood.

Course and subtypes. Symptoms may begin immediately or soon after the trauma. It is not unusual, however, for the symptoms to emerge after a latency period of months or years following the trauma.

When the symptoms begin within six months of the trauma and have not lasted more than six months, the acute subtype is diagnosed, and the prognosis for remission is good. If the symptoms either develop more than six months after the trauma or last six months or more, the chronic or delayed subtype is diagnosed.

Impairment and complications. Impairment may either be mild or affect nearly every aspect of life. Phobic avoidance of situations or activities resembling or symbolizing the original trauma may result in occupational or recreational impairment. "Psychic numbing" may interfere with interpersonal relationships, such as marriage or family life. Emotional lability, depression, and guilt may result in self-defeating behavior or suicidal actions. Substance Use Disorders may develop.

Predisposing factors. Preexisting psychopathology apparently predisposes to the development of the disorder.

Prevalence. No information.

Sex ratio and familial pattern. No information.

Differential diagnosis. If an **Anxiety, Depressive,** or **Organic Mental Disorder** develops following the trauma, these diagnoses should also be made.

In **Adjustment Disorder,** the stressor is usually less severe and within the range of common experience; and the characteristic symptoms of Post-traumatic Stress Disorder, such as reexperiencing the trauma, are absent.

Diagnostic criteria for Post-traumatic Stress Disorder
A. Existence of a recognizable stressor that would evoke significant symptoms of distress in almost anyone.

B. Reexperiencing of the trauma as evidenced by at least one of the following:

(1) recurrent and intrusive recollections of the event
(2) recurrent dreams of the event
(3) sudden acting or feeling as if the traumatic event were reoccurring, because of an association with an environmental or ideational stimulus

C. Numbing of responsiveness to or reduced involvement with the external world, beginning some time after the trauma, as shown by at least one of the following:

(1) markedly diminished interest in one or more significant activities
(2) feeling of detachment or estrangement from others
(3) constricted affect

D. At least two of the following symptoms that were not present before the trauma:

(1) hyperalertness or exaggerated startle response
(2) sleep disturbance
(3) guilt about surviving when others have not, or about behavior required for survival
(4) memory impairment or trouble concentrating
(5) avoidance of activities that arouse recollection of the traumatic event
(6) intensification of symptoms by exposure to events that symbolize or resemble the traumatic event

SUBTYPES

Post-traumatic Stress Disorder, Acute

A. Onset of symptoms within six months of the trauma.

B. Duration of symptoms less than six months.

Post-traumatic Stress Disorder, Chronic or Delayed

Either of the following, or both:

(1) duration of symptoms six months or more (chronic)

(2) onset of symptoms at least six months after the trauma (delayed)

300.00 Atypical Anxiety Disorder

This category should be used when the individual appears to have an Anxiety Disorder that does not meet the criteria for any of the above specified conditions.

Index

By the year 2000, 2 out of 3 Americans could be illiterate.

It's true.

Today, 75 million adults... about one American in three, can't read adequately. And by the year 2000, U.S. News & World Report envisions an America with a literacy rate of only 30%.

Before that America comes to be, you can stop it... by joining the fight against illiteracy today.

Call the Coalition for Literacy at toll-free **1-800-228-8813** and volunteer.

Volunteer Against Illiteracy. The only degree you need is a degree of caring.

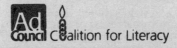

Ad Council Coalition for Literacy

Warner Books is proud to be an active supporter of the Coalition for Literacy.